BOB DUNWOODY
You Can Have It All

BOB DUNWOODY
You Can Have It All

By Robert C. Dunwoody

Let's Save America, Inc.

Let's Save America Inc.
Post Office Box 2869
Coeur d'Alene, ID 83816
800-372-1444

Library of Congress Cataloging-in-Publication Data
Library of Congress Control Number: 2002093607

Dunwoody, Robert C.
    Bob Dunwoody: You Can Have It All.

ISBN 0-9700067-1-3

[key words] 1. Success. 2. Success--Financial. 3. Success--Happiness. 4. Success--How to achieve. 4. Successful people. 5. Dunwoody. 6. Motivational speakers.

Acknowledgements

This book would never have been brought into existence
without the support, encouragement and enthusiasm of three
great people:

John Sherman, who began as my student
and became a teacher.

Brad Dugdale, whose focus, integrity and ability to create
gives joy to everyone who is fortunate enough
to be touched by him.

Karen Hayes, whose talent and professionalism are obvious,
and whose warmth and intuition are a blessing to all.

Thank you for coming into my life.

DEDICATION

As a student, I've had thousands of both "teachers" and "learners", all of whom have been of tremendous value to me. They've brought me to the path and supported me along the way.

Thank you all, from A to Z. You know who you are. I think of you often, and wish you joy.

I do want to mention, by name, those without whom my life would be empty.

Margie, my wife, buddy, and inspiration.
Laura, Bill, Sean — my children and their families, who provide a gift each day.
Kate,
Alex,
Simone,
Bill, Jr.,
and those grandchildren yet to come,
who each day "learn" me more about what it means to be human and show me how to live.

I love you all.

Table of Contents

Introduction

Thirty-five years ago, on the subway in New York City, it hit me: I was a failure.

I'd been a working man for about four years by that time, I had a wife and a small daughter, and I couldn't seem to get ahead, despite the fact that I was doing everything "right" – I was working two jobs, going in early, coming home late to a small apartment, and it seemed the harder I worked, the harder it was to make ends meet, let alone get ahead.

To make matters worse, my main job was in sales, and I hated it. As I sat there on the subway I realized that although I wanted to be able to pay my bills, what I wanted just as much—if not more—was to quit that job. The more I thought about it, the truer it felt.

Trouble was, I couldn't allow myself to quit a failure. So before the subway arrived at my stop, I made an agreement with myself: I decided that within two years I would be within the top 10% of the sales force… and THEN I'd quit! It wasn't as satisfying as quitting right then and there, but it was a plan I could agree to.

More importantly, it was a *vision:* walking into my boss's office and saying, "Take this job and shove it." Just having a destination, a road map out of that gerbil wheel of running faster and getting nowhere, made me feel better already. I was determined to see it through.

But how? Clearly I didn't know how to be successful, or I wouldn't be having this conversation with myself. I'd done all the right things, followed all the rules, and here I was. A failure. The only thing I knew for sure was that *what I was doing wasn't working.* I had to try something *different.* But what?

I decided to stop listening to the old rules and talk to some real experts: people who were successful in the field. So, I did an outrageous thing.

I called 75 of the top salesmen in Manhattan and said something along the lines of, "Hi, I'm a failure, I understand you're one of the best in your field, I wonder if I could meet

> **WHAT WE WERE TAUGHT**
>
> Success is a ladder. Unless you're born into a successful situation, you have to start at the bottom. Gradually, through self sacrifice and hard work, rung by rung, you'll work your way up to the top.

> "How did you become so successful in sales?"
>
> (Shrugs) "I don't know."
>
> "Did you work longer hours than everybody else?"
>
> "…No, I don't think so. Do you?"
>
> "Forget about me, I'm a failure. What do you say to prospective clients? How do you interest them?"
>
> "Um… I don't know, I just talk to them I guess. How do you do it?"

with you and maybe learn what I'm doing wrong."

Sounds ridiculous, I know, but most of these people were very nice. They didn't seem particularly taken aback by my bold request — in fact, many of them seemed somewhat intrigued — and they made time for me in their busy schedules. Thus began my education.

If I expected a light bulb to go off within the first five meetings, if I expected to see a common thread connecting these people, some combination of language and technique, some trick to success, I was in for a disappointment. None of them seemed to know why they were successful any more than I knew why I was a failure. One month into this project I was very discouraged—I began to think I would fail at this, too. But I am nothing if not persistent. I kept scheduling meetings, and eventually a pattern did begin to emerge.

There *were* some things these successful people all had in common. They just weren't the things I'd expected, so I hadn't been paying attention to the right clues. Truth is, the salesmen themselves were unaware of them, too. I sharpened my focus and kept interviewing. I learned enough in the next few months to convince myself the pattern was real. Then, I began to apply what I learned to my own work.

It made all the difference. In two years I achieved my goal. Did I quit? Well, there's an old saying that we love to do the things we're good at. It's true. I stayed, happily, for seven more years before moving to my next position as branch manager at a small office in Rochester, New York.

Of course I was thrilled with my success. But I wondered — was this just one of those weird formulas that worked for me but wouldn't work for anybody else? I decided to "inflict" my ideas onto the people in my department, and in just a couple years I had my answer. Our office went from a sales ranking of about 100th in the region… to within the top 20.

Again I moved on, this time managing a 4,000-man sales force, applying the same principles, with a bit more confidence. And, with the same success. I was definitely onto something.

There were some things these successful people all had in common. They just weren't the things I'd expected...

be a better human

It's been over 35 years since my "subway revelation". In that time I've exposed and shared the "technology of success" with literally thousands of people, making adjustments and refinements to my ideas. As I've gained experience I've been able to look back with a keener eye and catch a few points I'd missed along the way.

I discovered that the same ideas that helped build successful salespeople are applicable to just about every endeavor in life. They can help you be a better professional, a better plumber, a better spouse. They can help you improve your relationships, at home, in the workplace, and in the community. They can help you be a better parent, neighbor, partner, dog trainer, nanny. *They can help you be a better human.*

Sounds crazy, right? Read on, there are lots of "crazy" ideas in this book, crazy simply because they're different. It'll take you, at most, two uninterrupted hours to finish reading. Those two hours will be one of the best investments you've made in years.

Chapter 1
Who Are You?

Before we go any farther, I want you to ask yourself the same four questions I asked myself about 15 years ago, when my employer asked me to move to Chicago. (I declined and "retired".) Go ahead and write down your answers, without over-thinking. Allow yourself no more than 3 minutes to answer all the questions.

Don't overthink. 3 minutes only, for all 4 questions.

Who am I? _____

_____

Why do I get up every morning? _____

_____

What am I intending to accomplish? _____

_____

_____

What stands between me and success? _____

_____

> "Most men live lives of quiet desperation."
>
> Thoreau

Don't feel badly if you're dissatisfied with your answers—as you read this book, they're probably going to change. That's part of the fun of learning: looking back at what you believed to be true before you learned something new.

For many people, perhaps including yourself, the quick answer to question #1 is a checklist of your title, your circumstances, and your stuff:

1. I'm a computer programmer (or a CEO, or whatever),
2. I'm the second oldest of my siblings,
3. I've got a nice house,
4. a reliable car,
5. a college degree,
6. a neat new pair of skis,
7. a spouse I love,
8. two great children,
9. a stereo with surround-sound, and
10. a good dog.

As for *why you get up every morning*, odds are it's to get to work, so you can make the money you need to pay for that nice house and reliable car and wicked sound system, make the payments on the educational loan you had to take out for that college degree, keep food on the table and shoes on the kids, and so forth.

And *what you're trying to accomplish* probably goes something like this: I'm trying to get a raise, so I can get a nicer house, a hotter car, a big-screen TV, a snowmobile…. You get the idea.

So… are you your stuff? Is that who you are? Don't get me wrong—I like stuff. Stuff is nice. But what if something happens and you lose all your stuff… who are you then?

Are you your circumstances? Are you your job? "I'm a banker." "I'm a veterinarian." "I'm a city planner." Is that who you are? What if you lose your job… who are you then?

Are you a leaf in the wind, whose station in life is dictated by things over which you have little or no control?

> What if something happens and you lose all your stuff? What if you lose your job? Who are you then?

Something's missing….

...questions...

space of the

...live in the

Something's missing, isn't it?

These are the thoughts that ran through my head when I decided to "retire", and even though I was having trouble answering the questions, they made me realize I'd spent most of my then-50 years of life not really knowing who I was or why I was here.

It's okay. These are some of the toughest questions you'll have to grapple with in your life, and although you'll have to answer them in a way that satisfies you if you want to be a success, don't expect to do it right this minute. It took me a while, too. For now, just *live in the space of the questions* as you read on. Let them hover in your consciousness, so you're aware of them, but let's continue. The answers will show up.

As I mulled over the information I'd gleaned from my interviews with successful people, I realized that we all acquire information in two ways as we go through life:

We're *taught*,

and we're *learned*.

When you're *taught* something, someone purposely sets out to convey some specific information, such as *2 + 2 = 4*, or *look both ways before you cross the street.*

When someone *learns* you, you're picking up the information from them by an entirely different avenue—it's not something that's deliberately, consciously taught; it's more like something (good or bad) that rubs off on you as you go through life, and it's possible neither you nor the teacher is aware that the learning took place. Certain prejudices, for example, and belief systems—generally you aren't *taught* these things; you're *learned* them.

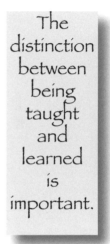

The distinction between being taught and learned is important.

This may sound like splitting hairs, but the distinction between being taught and being learned is important. When you are taught something, and subsequently a piece of information shows up to disprove what you were taught, you quickly change your thought process. When you are "learned" something, you will tend to cling to that, in spite of facts. In fact, we have codified our response—

SUCCESS IS LIKE RIDING A BIKE

If you ask a kid how to ride a 2-wheeled bike, he'll shrug and say, "Just get on and pedal." There are subtle ways he shifts his weight and moves the handlebars to balance, but it's not something he can dissect and teach. That's how it is with intuitively successful people. They've achieved this extraordinary thing— success— but they can't identify the subtle differences that brought them, but not the next person, to succeed.

"That's the exception that proves the rule"—and we don't even notice that the rule is invalid.

When you become aware of the fact that you've been picking up information almost accidentally, you can become more selective about what you'll allow yourself to absorb in the future, and what you'll reject. Just as importantly, you can look back on some of the belief systems you've been carrying around with you, unawares, and pull them out. Discard them, if they don't serve you.

There are good reasons for doing this, which I'll get into in a moment. For now, it's enough to know that by becoming aware of the inadvertent learning that takes place every day, YOU will be the one who decides what you believe, and what kind of person you are. You won't simply let it happen while you "sleep" anymore.

Who do you think has the most to learn? Successful people? Or people who are struggling to succeed? If you're already successful, don't you already know a lot about success?

That's what I used to think. But, as

I was beginning to figure out, most successful people weren't any more on the ball than anybody else.

They did not, on a conscious level, know *why* they were successful. As a result, they weren't particularly good at teaching others how to be successful. They couldn't identify what it was they'd done that got them where they were. They were ***intuitively successful***.

Not me. I had to study it. Hard. By consciously studying successful people, I learned things about them even they weren't conscious of. I discovered they weren't smarter than people who weren't successful. They weren't necessarily more skilled than people who hadn't succeeded. They hadn't necessarily worked harder—in fact, if anything they worked *less*. And, it wasn't dumb luck that handed them the brass ring.

I learned, by studying successful people, that they truly did things *differently* than most everybody else did, but not because they knew it was a better way. It was just intuitive for them. They weren't even conscious of it, or of how they were doing it. They couldn't explain it.

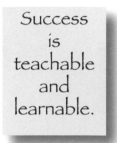
Success
is
teachable
and
learnable.

Success is not intuitive for most of us. Instead of being born with the ability to succeed, I learned how. I became *learned* about success by studying its nuts and bolts. And, as a result, I can teach it to you. Success is teachable and learnable.

Chapter 2

Characteristics of Successful People

Do successful people look different? I don't think so. Do they carry themselves differently or wear designer clothing? Not necessarily.

Do they have a distinguished vocabulary, or superior study skills? Not any more so than people who believe success is unachievable.

Are successful people the ones that got good grades in school? No, being a good student doesn't hurt, but despite what your guidance counselor might have told you in high school, good grades don't guarantee success in life, and a strong percentage of truly successful people made lousy grades in school.

Do they have charming personalities? No, I haven't found this to be a consistent factor, either.

> If successful people are no different than you or me, how come they're successful and we're not?

Do successful people "come from money?" This, too, seems to have nothing to do with it – many of the most successful people in the world came from humble beginnings. And if you're thinking poverty is the key, sparking the drive to succeed, sorry, but that's not the answer, either.

These were some of the first things I looked for in my interviews of successful people, and in my search for common threads I came up empty.

> Intuitively successful people do things differently, and they don't even know that they do things differently.

Then I did one of the smartest things I've ever done: I stopped thinking I knew what to look for.

And there it was — the answer. It had been there all along, waiting for me to open my mind, to stop being steered by my preconceived notions.

There are three major characteristics that tie all successful people together and change the way they see the world.

> There it was—the answer.
>   It had been there all along.

#1
Successful people are open to possibilities.

It took me several months to see this in the successful people I interviewed. Once I became aware of it, it was evident even in casual conversations with them, conversations that had nothing to do with business.

Successful people *live* in the world of possibilities. When presented with an idea, their intuitive response is, "Sounds crazy... Might work!"

Sounds crazy... Might work!

Most people live, instead, in the world of *options*.

Options don't sound so bad, right? What's wrong with living in the world of options? How do options stand in the way of success? What's the difference between living in the world of *possibilities*, versus living in the world of *options*?

The difference is in the *belief systems* that underlie each of those two worlds. Think of your belief systems as rocks you carry around with you in a backpack, influencing every decision you make. Everybody has them. We were *learned* our belief systems—they rubbed off on us—and we'll have the opportunity to add more of them to our backpacks as we go through life.

Here's one:

Knowledge Is Power.

Here's another:

It Takes Hard Work And Sacrifice To Succeed.

And another:

You Have To Start At The Bottom To Make It To The Top.

People who live in the world of *options* have a lot more belief systems like these — heavy rocks — in their backpacks, weighing them down, telling them what they can't do, what's impossible, and how things have to be "just because".

People who live in the world of *possibilities* are burdened with significantly fewer rocks. They travel light. And, as a result, they travel a lot farther, with a lot less energy expended. If this sounds to you like a nice philosophy that has no practical value, do yourself a favor:

Allow yourself to be open to the possibility that this book might teach you something you can apply to your life, to help you achieve the success that's been eluding you thus far.
Read on!

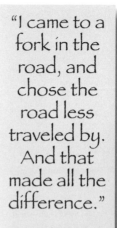

"I came to a fork in the road, and chose the road less traveled by. And that made all the difference."

Robert Frost

Options are pre-set, already defined. They're like rules that can't be broken, or lines in a coloring book.

What belief system were you *learned* when you got your first coloring book?

Stay inside the lines!

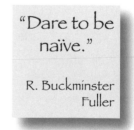

"Dare to be naïve."

R. Buckminster Fuller

Over time, people gather a lot of rocks like that one. When faced with a problem, they look in their ready-made backpack of options for the solution. Usually, there are lots of options, but if the *solution* isn't in there (and often it isn't), they're

Multi-Tasking At An Early Age

One early morning I saw a young boy on a bicycle, delivering newspapers. What made the scene less like a Norman Rockwell painting was the fact that the boy was wearing headphones connected to some device in his pocket, and while piloting the bike and tossing the papers he was playing a computer game. Where was his mind? Everywhere. And nowhere.

going to fail. And, they're going to waste a lot of energy, and suffer a lot of frustration, in the process, because they'll keep going through that backpack, trying the same things over and over, with no hope of success. It's exhausting, and demoralizing. It keeps people very busy, running around and around, getting nowhere. It's what "multi-tasking" is — doing several things, badly. Keeping several gerbil wheels spinning, getting nothing done.

Possibilities are endless. When you live in the world of possibilities, you approach problems with a boundless array of possible solutions. You're not limiting yourself to a backpack full of heavy, pre-set options. Remember, successful people lug around fewer belief systems. They travel light. You not only can go a lot farther, with a lot less energy wasted, when you travel light — you've also got a much greater *possibility of succeeding.*

For an example of how you, too, are limited by the world of options, take a look at the Puzzle Of Nine Dots, on the next page.

The Puzzle of 9 Dots
Connect all the dots with 4
straight lines without removing the
tip of your pen from the paper.
(Go ahead and solve it!)

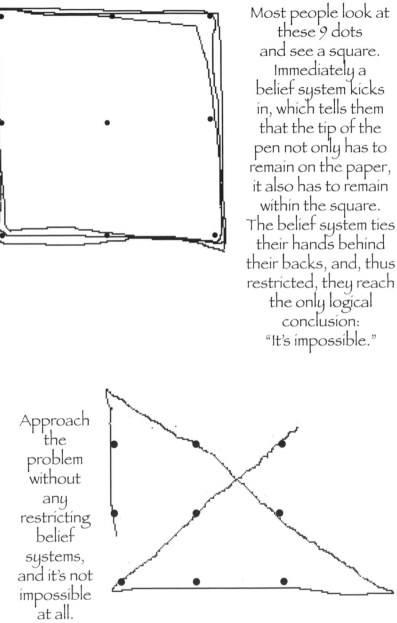

Most people look at these 9 dots and see a square. Immediately a belief system kicks in, which tells them that the tip of the pen not only has to remain on the paper, it also has to remain within the square. The belief system ties their hands behind their backs, and, thus restricted, they reach the only logical conclusion: "It's impossible."

Approach the problem without any restricting belief systems, and it's not impossible at all.

ONE WOMAN'S POSSIBILITIES

A 20-year-old woman in Colorado dropped out of college. Her reason: she wanted to live in a million-dollar home in the mountains, surrounded by servants, and spend her time skiing, hiking, and hanging out with movie stars and wealthy people.

Her mother outlined the options available to her:

> 1. Go back to school, get a good job, work hard for 20 or 30 years and accumulate a lot of money.

> 2. Marry a wealthy man who wants the same things.

Instead, she explored the possibilities.

She found out that most of those big, beautiful houses were empty 8 months of the year. The owners were worried about the houses when they were empty, and worried also that the cook, housekeeper, and gardener would not keep the houses in perfect shape...

She found a school with a one-year curriculum, teaching people how to run a big house and manage the staff. She graduated first in her class.

She was immediately hired by one of those families, and at the age of 24 her living situation is as follows:

She lives in a million-dollar home.
She is surrounded by servants.
She spends most of her time skiing, hiking, and spending time with her friends, some of whom are among the most prominent people in the country.
She is also very well paid.

That's the difference between OPTIONS and POSSIBILITIES.

Do successful people have more time?

Of course not. But how many times have you heard the lament, "If only I had more time….," from people struggling to succeed, while at the same time you see successful people getting more done? If they don't have more time, how do they do it?

Here's how. We all have the same amount of time. But a select few of us use our time differently.

Successful people don't use their time exhausting themselves.

For the rest of us, living in the restricted world of options is just about all we're able to accomplish, then we run out of time and energy.

Here's a novel idea: Perhaps working harder is not the answer to success! Perhaps part of the answer is to SLOW DOWN. Sounds crazy, right? Might work.

As we progress, I'll show you exactly how to slow down.

Most of us are too busy.

Being busy is not required. Being productive is the key to success. We are too busy doing things that are not productive. It is not always necessary to be busy in order to be productive!

Belief System:
You must be busy to be productive.

"I don't know where we're headed, but we're making great time."

Yogi Berra

"A fair wind does not help a sailor who has no destination."

Heraclitus

#2
Successful people are conscious.

Successful people have a tremendous advantage over other people: They are "conscious".

That probably sounds ridiculous. Of course, everybody is conscious! But not everybody is as aware of what's going on around them as successful people are.

For example, most of us don't notice change until it hits us between the eyes, and then we react to it. As a result, we're constantly playing the game of catch-up, which is a stressful game, and not much fun.

It's akin to being cut off on a high-speed roadway, and having to veer suddenly to avoid a collision, or deal with the crumpled bumper and personal injuries that follow if you don't react quickly enough.

Successful people see change coming, and they make adjustments accordingly, ahead of time, so they're ready for it when it comes. Instead

> "It takes a person who is wide awake to make his dreams come true."
>
> Roger Babson

of reacting with dangerous, sudden moves, they use foresight, they change lanes, or turn onto a different road. In the marketplace, as in life, this gives them a valuable edge.

There are other advantages to being conscious, and they're integral to your ability to be successful in life. More on that in a moment.

Meanwhile, how do successful people stay conscious? It's simple: They are constantly aware that there is a lot they don't know. That's right, successful people believe they know LESS than other people, successful or not. To understand this, you have to understand the next characteristic of successful people: They Know What They Don't Know. Read on!

> Successful people "know" LESS than people who are not successful.

#3
Successful people know what they don't know.

You probably thought successful people know a lot more than you do. I thought so too, 30 years ago. They would disagree.

We are taught in life that knowledge is power—that's one of the more common belief systems we tend to carry around in our backpacks. We're taught to pad our resumés and present ourselves as though we know a lot about a lot of things. But consider this:

> People who know everything are the least likely to be successful.

Here's why.

You have three different kinds of knowledge:

1. What you know you know.
All the things you're <u>sure of</u> would go into this category (even if they're WRONG!).

2. What you know you don't know.
This category includes all the things you don't know, as far as you're aware. I know that I don't know how to fly a jet, for example. I know that I don't know how to perform brain surgery. I don't know how to make a soufflé. What I don't know is a pretty big list.

T or F:

Knowledge is Power

(false!)

> When you
> know you
> know there
> are no
> possibilities,
> then there
> are only
> options
> within the
> constraints
> of what you
> know.

3. What you don't know you don't know.

This is the largest category. It includes all the things about which you're totally oblivious. You're not even aware that these things exist.

Which of these three categories of "knowing" represents the power position?

If you subscribe to the belief system that says *Knowledge Is Power*, you'll pick #1. That's the one most people choose. People who are not successful, that is.

The position of power is #2: *Knowing what you don't know*. Here's why.

When you're doing something you've done a hundred times, odds are you could do it in your sleep. Have you ever started feeling drowsy, or actually fallen asleep, while driving your car on a familiar route? It's very common. You go unconscious. You go on auto-pilot. Many people actually engage in multi-tasking while they're driving — they shave, put on makeup, dial their cell phones, read a map, eject a CD, put it in its case, find another one, open the case, pop it into the slot: So confident are they in their ability to drive that they relegate it — handling a 3,000+ pound vehicle at 70 miles an hour on a busy expressway — to the back of their minds, while they do something else.

But what if you're driving in an unfamiliar area, where you don't feel confident, or even safe? Your eyes are wide open, your mind is uncluttered, and you're concentrating on every street sign, every pedestrian, every detail of getting from point A to point B. You're wide awake. You make an effort to be *fully conscious*, because you're aware that you're in unfamiliar territory. *You know that you don't know* your way around. You *know that you don't know* the territory, and you're concerned about missing a turn, or colliding with a pedestrian. Because you're wide awake, the odds of making such an error are vastly reduced.

That's how successful people navigate through life, even the day-to-day stuff: They intuitively know that they *don't know everything*. They intuitively believe that every day and every task are new, with endless

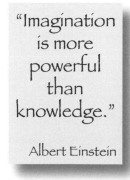

"Imagination is more powerful than knowledge."

Albert Einstein

"The only thing that we can know is that we know nothing and that is the highest flight of reason."

Leo Tolstoy

possibilities. And so, they make the effort to remain fully conscious, in order to not miss something valuable.

There are tremendous benefits to knowing what you don't know, and when you operate from a "not knowing" point of view, your behavior changes in many ways.

> Most people who know all the answers seldom ask the correct questions.

For example, in addition to going unconscious, most people who "know" feel obligated to play Know And Tell. I'll bet you're acquainted with many people who always have strong opinions about things, always know everything, and are always telling you what you're doing wrong, even though they're clearly less successful than you are.

Successful people, on the other hand, don't play Know And Tell. Even the intuitively successful people I interviewed in Manhattan, who weren't aware they were doing it, were playing Ask And Listen, operating from a position of *knowing what they don't know*. As they sat in their corner offices filled with the evidence of their success, they asked *me* how *I* did things, and were genuinely interested in my answers, because they were open to the possibility that I might have an idea or angle they hadn't considered. They didn't believe that as successful people, they automatically knew everything, and that I, a failure, knew nothing. They unburdened themselves of that belief system, or heavy rock, and kept their minds *open to the possibilities.* Think of any person you know who is clearly unsuccessful. Odds are, that's a person who knows everything about everything, and is always telling you how much he knows. Odds are, that's a person who goes unconscious and never does anything differently, year after year, even if the way he does things has not served him.

This applies to everything in life, including your relationships. Think of your most intimate relationship, with your significant other. Think back to how it was when you first became interested in each other. You knew nothing about that person. You spent hours and hours asking a lot of questions about each other, and listening to the answers. You were *exploring the possibilities*! A relationship developed, and it was exciting and fresh, because you *knew what you didn't know.*

"What good are computers, they just give answers. The power is in asking the right question."

Pablo Picasso

Now you've been together for some time, and what do you know about that person? *"Everything!"* You know so much about that person that you don't even have to talk to each other any more, right? You don't have those great conversations you had in the beginning. You know how he or she is going to respond if you express your thoughts and feelings, so you save yourself the effort. You know how he or she thinks and feels about things, so you don't ask, or listen.

You've riddled your relationship with belief systems!

You've switched from *Ask & Listen* to *Know & Tell.*

You're no longer *open to the possibilities.* You've denied that person, and yourself, and your relationship, the possibility of growth and change. You've gone unconscious.

The bottom line about "knowing" is that it eliminates *possibilities* and replaces them with *options.*

If "knowing" is "bad," is it "good" to be "ignorant?" Of course not. There is a difference between *knowing* and *having knowledge.* The difference is, despite the knowledge they've acquired with study and experience, successful people never assume they know *everything*, and they remain open to the possibility that there is always *more* to learn, even in the activities they do every day, even in the relationships in which they live. *They know what they don't know.* That's the position of *power* and *success.*

Insanity: Doing the same thing over and over, and expecting different results.

The Laws of Success

In addition to being open to the possibilities, being fully conscious, and remaining unfettered by an inflated sense of "knowing," successful people also follow three immutable, universal laws. No matter what you want to do, have, or be, you must obey these laws if you truly want to be successful. They are as follows:

Have your integrity in place at all times.

Everybody makes mistakes, including successful people. Rather than cover up and carry that burden around in their backpacks, successful people admit their mistakes, clean up the mess they've made, and move on with

> "The greatest discovery of my generation is that human beings can alter their lives by altering their attitudes of mind."
>
> William James

a lightened load. Not only is this the right choice morally, philosophically, and legally, it's also the only path to true success.

Be technically competent.

If you want to be a successful engineer, doctor, or garbage collector, if you want to be in a fabulous relationship —you must understand what makes a "good" performer. There is no shortcut for this, and adhering to it gives you the tools you need to obey law #3:

Add value.

Approach every endeavor with the aim of making a meaningful contribution. Most people come from the opposite direction: How can I get as much as possible out of this situation, with the least amount of effort on my part? Instead, aim to be the one who *adds* to the equation. For many, this seems exactly the opposite of what would be logical. And they're right: Success is not logical. Success is counterintuitive.

SUCCESS IS COUNTERINTUITIVE

Chapter 3
What Is Success To You?

In our culture, success is all about "stuff," and "more". We're marinated in these definitions of success every day. There are some fabulously wealthy people in this world who work themselves into the ground because they always want more. What they have is never enough.

If you always want "more," you're playing a game that can never be won: there will always be *more*. If you play the "stuff" game — if for you, success is measured by the stuff you acquire — then you've set yourself up for ultimate frustration: "stuff" never changed anything. "Stuff" never made anybody happy, not in a lasting way.

If our society's definitions of success—"more" and "stuff"—aren't

> The "more" game can never be won: there will always be more.

> The "stuff" game sets you up for chronic frustration: stuff never brings lasting happiness.

37

valid, then does success exist? Can it be defined?

It can. And, you can use its definition right now, to determine whether you're already successful. Here's how.

Let's say your god, whatever universal power you believe in, wants to reward you, and offers to change anything about your life that you want changed—the quality of your relationships, for example, or the size of your bank account, or the value of the home you live in, or your golf handicap — anything you can think of that you'd like to be different than it is. And your response is, 'Thanks, God, but I'm happy with things the way they are."

That's success.

So... are you successful? Probably not, and it's not my intention to be demeaning. In my experience, only about 3% of the people in this country are truly successful, so it's a safe bet you're among the remaining 97%. To switch teams and get into the successful 3% requires some insight into what would be required for you to say "Thanks, God, but I'm happy

So...
are you
successful?

Probably not.

with things the way they are." What would it take?

It's not as easy as it sounds. People have a lot of trouble with this question, because some heavy belief systems stand in the way.

"You Can't Have It All," says one belief system.

"Life Is A Series Of Tradeoffs," says another.

"Do you want to have a lot of money?… Or do you want to be a good parent? You Can't Have It All!"

"Do you want to have a profitable job?… Or do you want to have fun? You Can't Have It All!"

I disagree. It's true that you can't have *everything,* but there's every possibility you can have it all.

First you have to define what "it all" is for you. It's different for everybody, but you can figure it out pretty easily.

It's true that you can't have everything, but there's every possibility that you can have it all.

In fact, it's a question only you can answer. Here's how:

Give Yourself The Gift Of Ten Minutes.

This exercise will take ten minutes, tops. Set aside this time for yourself. Make sure you'll not be interrupted — no telephone, no beeper, no accountability, unloaded of all burdens and responsibilities, for ten precious minutes. Make it happen. It'll be well worth it. To this 10-minute haven, bring a pad of paper and a pen, nothing more.

List everything you want. If you have any belief systems standing in your way, telling you this exercise isn't practical or healthy, dismiss those belief systems from the room and start writing. Be honest and specific about what you really want — don't just write, "I want more money" — specify how much you want, and when. Don't just write, "I want to feel better" — specify what you mean by "better," and what it'd take to make you feel that way.

And again, don't let yourself be influenced by belief systems or by what others might say—this is a private conversation.

For some of you reading this, right this minute, the following thoughts are showing up:

"When is this going to get real?"
"I'm too old for this!"
"This is a waste of time."

Don't you see? Those are your belief systems determining your behavior. They won't even allow you to take ten minutes to explore the possibilities for your life. Don't let them have that much power. Take your time, and see this exercise through.

Finished?
If you're like most people, there are about ten to fifteen things on your list.

Now circle all items on the list to which you are truly committed—this separates them from those "gee it would be nice" things that you'd enjoy but you wouldn't be willing to pay for, or work for, or take as a substitute. This is an important step, because what "gee it would be nice" things do is detour you from your

For some of you reading this, right this minute, the following thoughts are showing up:

"When is this going to get real?"
"I'm too old for this!"
"This is a waste of time."

Your belief systems won't even give you 10 minutes to explore a possibility.

41

"A 5 handicap in golf ...."

"Double my income ...."

"Be the head of my department...."

"Go on a date once a week with my spouse..."

"Lose 15 pounds."

"Achieve Level II Dressage with my horse ...."

"Lower my total cholesterol to 185...."

"Learn to speak French...."

"Be a better parent...."

"Buy a new TV...."

commitments, which is what much of the advertising in this society aims to get you to do.

Finished? How many have you got? Most people circle three to five things on their lists; the rest are things that are in the "gee it would be nice" category.

How difficult was that, ultimately?

If you're like most people, it's difficult to get *started* writing down the things you want in life, because your belief systems keep you from even thinking along these lines — they tell you that by identifying your at-the-top goal, instead of first making a plan and working up from the bottom, you're setting yourself up for disappointment, frustration, and failure.

And, if you're a woman, one of your belief systems probably tells you that you aren't valid unless you sacrifice your dreams in order to care for others — it's "self centered" to think of your own wants, and that's "unattractive".

These rocks in your backpack can be more like boulders, and for many women it's a little tough to get around them. Once you do it, however, you'll be forever changed. That's good.

Circling the items to which you're committed is also difficult for many people, because *commitment* is a dirty word in our society. It's something our culture discourages, sometimes in jest, sometimes in all seriousness. Our belief systems tell us commitment is a straitjacket. Commitment boxes you in.

> Commitment is the needle on a compass. All it does is provide guidance.

In fact, the opposite is true. Commitment is the needle on a compass. All it does is provide guidance.

Whether you heed that guidance is entirely up to you. A compass never scolds or passes judgment, it never threatens or laughs at you. The choice is yours. You can change the direction in which you're moving, or you can change your commitments.

> "Commit. Until you commit, you're just taking up space."
>
> Gary Cooper
> (High Noon)

At the very least, you'll be aware that you're on the right path, or not. This already is a big improvement for most of us, who may not even have known (or acknowledged) what our goals were, and may have been making life choices day after day without being conscious of whether they're keeping

COMMITMENTS

us on track or pulling us off course.

By making the list, and circling your commitments, you achieve three things:

•1. You *change your mindset* and bring the things you want into view — these are things that may not even have been on your radar screen at all until you identified them.

•2. Circling the items to which you're committed helps keep you *focused* on those things, and helps you differentiate them from the "gee it would be nice" things that divert you from your commitments.

•3. You can see clearly that most of the things that *keep you busy* are either in the "gee" category, or they're not even on the list at all! No wonder success seems so far away!

You may have noticed you also became *relaxed*.

It happens to everybody when they envision their ultimate goals from the top. A practical voice might tell you "It'll never happen," but another voice says, "… but if it did…" and a smile appears on your face.

Most of the things that keep you busy are "gee-it-would-be-nices".

44

Intuitively successful people do exactly what you just did. But they do it regularly, in order to update themselves on how they're doing and to make adjustments in their list according to how their vision has changed.

And, they do it without pen and paper. In their minds they know what they want, ultimately. They start at the top. They're not at all uncomfortable creating in their heads a picture of the house they want, the job they want, the mate they want, etc., and they're not at all intimidated by the prospect of setting out to find those things, instead of settling for what's available when they happen to be looking. Great world leaders do the same.

History's great visionaries always started at the top.

What about that belief system that tells us we should start with a plan, rather than a vision?

History, and the great visionaries that created it, would give that idea a flip-flop. Start at the top. Start at the end of the game. That means *start with a vision.*

By giving yourself the Gift Of Ten Minutes, you've done exactly that, and you've opened the door for an amazing cascade of events:

WORK FROM
THE TOP
DOWN:

VISIONS

lead to

PLANS

which create

STRATEGIES

which lead to

TACTICS.

1. Once you have a *vision*, a *plan* appears.
2. Once you're conscious of the plan, an appropriate *strategy* becomes obvious.
3. Once you've got a strategy, the daily *tactics* become apparent to you.

If you start at the top, *you will be aligned with your vision.* This is what successful people do. *Aligned* is what successful people are. They resist being pulled, pushed, knocked, or otherwise distracted off course for any significant length of time.

Most of us are *misaligned*, because we are unclear about our vision. If we are unclear about our vision, how can we know if we are on course? How can we have a useful plan?

Visions create possibilities.
Visions do not have time frames.
Visions give you a "way to travel" which is just as important as the destination.
The problem with merely having a plan, unaccompanied by a vision, is that it doesn't allow you to notice possibilities to achieve your vision

when they appear—you're too busy implementing your plan.

A plan with no vision often feels like a burden, a "have to".

A vision feels like an open door.

Give The Ultimate Gift

Now that you have your list, and your vision, go to your significant other—the person with whom you have a long term relationship — and give him or her the Gift Of Ten Minutes. Provide a blank sheet of paper, a pen, the same instructions I gave you, and ten minutes of uninterrupted private time. When he or she is finished, sit down together and share your lists, especially the visions — the items you each circled.

You'll have one of the greatest conversations you've ever had with that person, greater even than the conversations you had early in the relationship, when you both were asking questions and listening to the answers.

Why greater? Because each of you is sharing your visions — your life goals — with a person who knows you

We spend time, effort, energy, and emotions pursuing things others say we "should" have. A simple way to get "un-busy:" stop "efforting" for things you don't want. Get CONSCIOUS about the things to which you are committed.

better, and cares more about you, than anybody else does. And, by opening up this dialogue with your significant other, you are shifting the relationship from a position of "knowing" to a position of "not knowing". You are both becoming conscious again. Open to the possibilities.

And, the icing on the cake: After you've shared your visions with each other, look your significant other in the eyes and say, "I give you my word that I will support you in honoring your commitments." In all likelihood, you will receive the same vow in return (but don't expect it – let there be no strings attached). Then, be open to the possibility that this exercise will create a dynamic in your relationship that had gotten lost. Gone unconscious.

And, returning to the three immutable laws of success, you are adding *value* to this relationship.

You are back on course.

"It's not the mountain we conquer but ourselves."

Sir Edmund Hillary

Chapter 4
Why Do People
Go To Work?

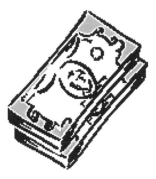

Well, that's simple: To make money, right? That's the way most employers and employees see it—it's part of our belief system.

Salesmen are paid a commission for making sales, so it's clear that whoever set up that system believes that the extra money is what motivates a salesman to sell. Bonuses are paid at the end of the year to employees who have achieved a certain level of production. Whoever set up that system believes, too, that the bonus money is the motivator for high production.

But the statistics show that this system does not work. Not in the long run. The income of people who are paid on an incentive basis typically reaches a maximum in five to seven years, then levels out, even though the incentives are still in place—that extra money is still sitting out there, telling the employee that if he or she works harder, he or she can have more of it, as a reward.

So... if people go to work to earn money, why does performance plateau after five to seven years even when more money is there for the taking?

Quite simply, because people go *unconscious.*

We go unconscious because we lose our *motivation.*

We lose our motivation because in five to seven years, our *needs* have changed — and a little extra money no longer meets our needs.

That doesn't seem to mesh with what we're taught, does it. The message we receive in this society is that you can never have enough money. But this is not reality. For most people, money is a way to achieve comfort. And once you're comfortable, even though it's not the kind of comfort you dream of, your need for money is met. A need once met no longer motivates.

The only way to get around this is to understand what our needs are at any given time, and adjust the incentive

5 - 7 yrs

For most people, income flattens out at 5 - 7 years, even if they could earn more with improved performance.

A need once met no longer motivates.

so we stay conscious and motivated. Psychologist Abraham Maslow illustrated it beautifully with his "Hierarchy of Need".

To simplify Maslow's hypothesis, man is motivated by four basic needs which are met in a specific order, from lowest to highest:

1. Physiological needs (survival)
2. Love and belonging (comfort),
3. Self esteem (recognition), and
4. Self actualization (spiritual and existential issues).

Level I: Survival

A man who is dying of thirst on the desert would do most anything within reason for a glass of water. He's motivated by the first hierarchy of need: survival.

Once his thirst is quenched, he's less likely to do much of anything for a glass of water.

<u>A need once met no longer motivates you.</u>

Level II: Comfort

What is comfort? It is the reason most

people go to work every morning.

People work to get comfortable.

> Money is a primary motivator only when you don't have enough of it to be comfortable.

If money is what it takes to make you comfortable, then money will be your primary motivator only as long as you don't have enough of it to be comfortable. Because comfort is the only thing that motivates most people to perform at work, their work performance plateaus at five to seven years for one simple reason:

They've gotten comfortable.

Unless a new incentive arises, their work performance does the same thing as their income: it levels off. As work performers, they shut down. They go unconscious. They switch on the autopilot.

Now here's the really bad news:

Not only does being stuck at "comfort" seriously undermine people's ability to get ahead, it also sets them up for some sort of crisis, thanks to the Law Of Entropy :
THINGS GET WORSE.
It sounds harsh and fatalistic, but it's as reliable and unforgiving as the law of gravity.

Things get WORSE.

When we get comfortable and disengage, something pulls the rug out from under us and tumbles us back down into survival mode…

…which shifts us to the bottom of the hierarchy and renews our motivation.

We work hard, we get comfortable, we go unconscious, we hit bottom, and then we start all over again. We scratch and scramble to climb out of the hole and for a while our performance picks up. Then we get comfortable again, and things go south. "Life is tough" because we keep doing the tough part over and over and over. Read on and see how to stop this cycle.

Being comfortable is not the ceiling. It's the floor.

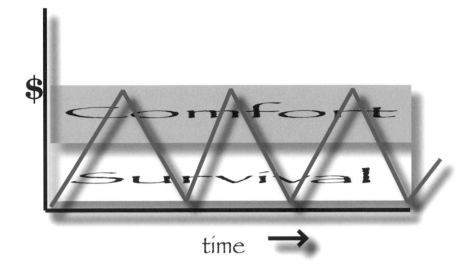

time →

> "Life is tough" because we keep doing the hard part over and over again.

To make matters worse, despite its predictability, some of our belief systems allow the Law Of Entropy to catch us by surprise every time. Here's a common one:

IF YOU DO IT RIGHT THE FIRST TIME, YOU WON'T HAVE TO DO IT AGAIN.

It doesn't matter who you learned it from, it's simply not true.

We're taught that we can fix things. The truth is, nothing of value is ever fixed permanently — everything worth having requires maintenance, whether it's a hot car, or a fancy house, or an intimate relationship.

54

As teenagers we were taught that once we got married, it'd be 'til death do us part.' That sounded pretty good, and we looked forward to the day when we could kick back.

What we didn't hear was that many relationships fail because people get comfortable, switch from a place of "not knowing" to one of "knowing," and fail to realize it takes work to keep that relationship alive and healthy. Your relationship, just as your car, will deteriorate unless you take good care of it.

For many of us, getting comfortable feels initially like we've "made it" — that comfort makes us want to kick back and relax; we're done.

We've gotten married, and now we don't have to work at the relationship any more; we're done.

We've landed a good job, and we don't have to work at selling ourselves any more; we're done.

We go unconscious.

With that mindset, we're fodder for the Law Of Entropy, which aims to

> Everything worth having requires maintenance, whether it's a hot car, or a fancy house, or an intimate relationship.

> "Every ceiling, when reached, becomes a floor."
>
> Aldous Huxley

knock us right out of our comfort zone… back down to survival mode. None of it would happen if we only understood the following truth:

Being comfortable is not the ceiling. It's the floor.

When you are in survival mode, there are NO possibilities.

When you achieve comfortableness, you have the choice to start *exploring the possibilities* and, by staying *conscious*, to start protecting yourself against the Law Of Entropy. Then, and only then, can you set your sites on higher visions.

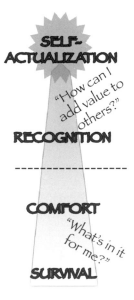

Level III: Recognition

If we're already comfortable, what is the next motivator? What, in other words, would we gladly work for?

Recognition, which feeds our self esteem and gives us confidence, a sense of worth, and the respect of others.

Money is one way people are recognized for the value they add to any endeavor. But it is not the only way, and by itself is certainly not

Recognition: A personal anecdote

I was thrown out of the first grade by the New York City school system. This is not an easy accomplishment.

I was considered disruptive, uncontrollable and unteachable. My mother would take me to school, and I'd run through the halls and be home before she arrived.

In desperation, it was arranged for me to attend a different school. That didn't bother me, because at age 6 I'd figured out how to beat the system.

I was escorted to the principal's office. Ms. Sands was the classical stereotype of a school principal in the 1940s. Gray hair, in a tight bun, a severe black dress and round glasses. She knew about my record, and I knew that she knew.

Ms. Sands smiled and asked me, "Which one of the 'Dunwoody boys' is your dad? I taught all of them. They were fine boys and good students."
At age 6, I thought my father's name was "Dad," My mother gave the answer.
"Cecil?" said Ms. Sands, "He was the best of all the boys. I bet you're just like him."
She escorted me to my classroom and told Ms. Donoughe that I was "Cecil's son" and to expect me to be a very good student.
From that moment on, I was.
A little recognition goes a long way.
This happened to me 62 years ago.
I'm sure Ms. Sands never realized what she had done for me in 10 minutes, by recognizing me.

She changed my life.

~ # ~

enough, nor is it a suitable substitute for the kind of kudos that raise our self esteem.

Ironically, recognition is in short supply in this society. In fact, when people are asked what makes them most dissatisfied with their jobs (including homemaking and raising the kids), almost all say they feel unappreciated and undervalued. In fact, when asked specifically which would make them happier in their jobs—more money or more recognition—more people identify *lack of recognition* as the underlying cause for their discontent. Their need for recognition is not met. In our society, there is a huge <u>demand</u> for recognition, and woefully inadequate <u>supply</u>.

In our society there is a huge DEMAND for recognition, and woefully inadequate SUPPLY.

How do people at work respond to a lack of recognition? They shut down. They become increasingly resentful. And, they stop trying. Frustrated in their desire for recognition, they *settle* for comfort — the paycheck — and they *give only as much as they have to* for it.

And then the Law Of Entropy kicks in once again.

Since 9/11, I spend a lot more time in airports because of beefed-up security. Most everybody agrees it's an inconvenience, but over time it's easy to lose sight of what the new security personnel are doing for us.

I appreciate the National Guardsmen, who are away from their families in order to make me feel safer. It's easy to forget that, when you're stressed and tired and trying to make connections.

So, one day I approached an officer and thanked him.

I meant it.

From the look on his face, it was clear that the recognition from those two tiny words — thank you — had made his day. It was also clear that he hadn't heard them very often.

Supply and demand. Huge demand, puny supply. We can change that so easily. Just start giving recognition away. Do it. You'll be amazed at the difference you'll make, for yourself as well as for the recipient.

Successful people know, intuitively, that one of the best ways to get recognition is to give it. It seems counterintuitive, but it's another law of nature, and it applies not only to recognition but to everything else in life, including love, money, inspiration, and so on. I call it the Law Of Abundance:

If You Think About What You Need Most In Life, And Give It Away, It Will Come Back To You Manyfold.

By the same token, when you really need money, it's tough to get it. But when you want something *bigger*— something that transcends money — money seems to arrive in boatloads.

In business, truly successful people do not look at a new idea or product and ask, "How much money can I make from this?" Instead, they first ask, "Will this idea or product impact other people's lives?" If the new venture <u>will</u> impact other lives, then

The Law Of Abundance

they know it will make a great deal of money.

Level IV: Self Actualization

Self actualization is what tells you who you are. It is the collection of goals that makes you as an individual feel fulfilled, both spiritually and in terms of your own potential. It is what gives life meaning for you.

Rather than being about what you want and need for yourself, it is about how you can positively impact the world. It is the jewel that makes life fulfilling. And, it is what gives you the answer to the tough questions I asked at the beginning of Chapter 1:

- Who am I?
- Why do I get up every morning?
- What am I trying to accomplish?

Self actualization is why fabulously successful people often become benefactors of worthy causes. Bill and Melinda Gates have already achieved the first three levels of motivation (survival, comfort, and recognition); they have chosen to work toward Level IV: making a difference. They have focused their efforts on providing education for disadvantaged children across the globe. Because of not only their wealth but also their *commitment* to this cause, they stand to make a profound difference in the world, while also achieving self actualization.

This is not to suggest that you have to be outrageously wealthy to achieve self actualization; you only have to be motivated to work at that level. And, for this to be possible, your needs for survival, comfort, and recognition must first be met. Your motivation changes along with your needs.

Unfortunately, many people spend their working years saving enough money to retire, and spending their retirement worrying whether they'll have enough money to remain comfortable — they're stuck at level II, and by the Law Of Entropy they're doomed to fall back into survival mode again and again. There also is a segment of our population that for one reason or another quits at level III (recognition), without ever attempting to make a difference in

NOT MUCH OF A RETIREMENT

~

People spend their working years saving enough money to retire, then spend their retirement worrying whether they'll have enough to stay comfortable. They're stuck at level II on the hierarchy of need.
By the Law Of Entropy they're doomed to fall back into survival mode again and again and again....

the world, striving only for fame and fortune for themselves.

Levels I and II are basically about *me* and *my needs*. With their vision focused inwardly in this way, for many people self actualization will remain outside their radar screen. They are likely to feel chronically unfulfilled, and their golden years are likely to seem empty.

> For people stuck at or below Level II, the "golden years" are likely to feel empty.

The vision turns outward, towards the needs of others, at Level III. Being in the upper tiers of the hierarchy brings a sense of having "lived life".

By becoming aware of the four levels of motivation, you give yourself an easy way to identify at which level you're residing at any given period of your life, no matter what is happening at the time, so you can understand why you're tending to make the choices you make.

Bad things will happen — nobody is immune — but what separates the successful people from the not-so-successful people is how long they stay in the lower tiers of the hierarchy before they dust themselves off and get back into the higher reaches of the climb.

By applying the four levels of motivation to every circled item on your list of visions, you have a better chance of staying conscious, which means you can see change coming before it knocks you off course. You can keep yourself motivated and aligned to your vision. You are better able to succeed, not only in your career, but in your relationships, your golf game — anything to which you have vowed your commitment.

Here's the joke:
When you work for money, it's tough to make money.
When you "work" to make a difference, you can't stop the money from showing up.

"If we did all the things we are capable of doing, we would literally astonish ourselves."

Thomas Edison

Chapter 5
How To Retire Now

In the last chapter, we explored the reasons why people work, and we learned why the most common answer — "for money" — doesn't hold water. Remember, most people work to get *comfortable* — to achicve level II on the motivation hierarchy. Getting comfortable takes a certain amount of money, to pay for food, housing, and "stuff," but for many people in the work setting it also requires that the job be as undemanding as possible. These people do everything they can to make their job *predictable* and get it *under control*. That way, they can go unconscious.

RETIRE
FIRST.
And then
make a lot of
money.

Why do they want this? I believe there are two reasons.

1. First, if they're like most people, they probably feel they're not getting enough *recognition* (motivation Level III). The truth is, they're probably right — there's very little recognition

> The "game" at work:
> Get the most output for the least input, then go unconscious.

to go around in this society (more on the reasons for that in a moment). For the majority of people in the work force, this scarcity of recognition becomes a sore point, and because it's their nature to blame some outside factor for their plight (rather than look inward for their own role in it), they become resentful. If they choose to believe there's nothing they can do to improve their self esteem, they become stuck at the second level of motivation, and they blame the job.

2. The second reason they go unconscious has to do with a game people play at work. The rules of the game are simple:

Do As Little As Possible, And Get As Much As Possible In Return.

Because people come to believe their job is the obstacle standing in the way of their lives, the game becomes the primary objective in the workplace. To achieve comfort, they work to get the most output for the least input, and then they go unconscious. This attitude can be contagious, like a virus.

Now, think of the attitude people take with them when they play. They never go unconscious. That's because the objective in play is to *WIN!* That's the game. Getting comfortable isn't part of the equation.

The sour attitude people tend to bring to work, compared to the vibrant, committed, give-200% attitude they bring to play, is common and fairly predictable. And, it reassures people that *their lack of success is not their fault* — it's the fault of the job — they're merely victims. Perhaps it's not the job that determines the attitude. Perhaps, instead, the attitude comes first, in the form of the rules that are learned and unconsciously carried into the workplace on the first day, then reinforced by coworkers.

It's no surprise that for many people, retirement becomes the ultimate goal. They retire for one reason: so they can *quit work*. Period. Ask them what they plan to do after retirement, and if they're honest, they'll realize the answer is: NOTHING. For them, retirement is simply the *absence of work*, and they don't look any farther than that — it's enough.

The "game" at play: WIN!

For many, retirement is simply the absence of work, and they don't look any farther than that.

The game for most people at work is DO AS LITTLE AS POSSIBLE, AND GET AS MUCH AS POSSIBLE IN RETURN. In play, the game is to WIN. With which attitude are we most likely to stay conscious? With which do you think you will be more likely to succeed?

But this sort of retirement is not likely to be very satisfying for very long. You can only fish for so many hours. You can only golf so much. Travel is nice, but it won't hold your interest indefinitely. Television? Forget it. So really. What *are* your plans for retirement?

Work At Being Retired

Successful people are retired long before they quit work, because their work is what they *want* to do, rather than something they feel they *have* to do in order to fulfill survival or comfort needs.

Bill Gates goes to work every morning because that's what he wants to do, certainly not because he needs to. Tom Hanks makes movies because there are good scripts out there, not because he needs the money. Yo-Yo Ma does concerts because he loves to play the cello, not because he has to work to pay bills.

I travel, away from the comfort of my home at an age when most people are "retired," because I love sharing what I've learned over 40 years, I love seeing the light of insight in people's faces when they "get" it, and I love the idea of making a difference. The money is great, but it's not what primarily motivates me. I'm putting in as many hours now as I did twenty years ago, working harder than my children would like me to, and in my mind I have been retired for a long, long time.

The trick is to discard the belief system that tells you that work is tough, nose to grindstone, shoulder to wheel, a daily grind we all *have* to subject ourselves to... so we can afford to play. Instead of thinking of work as a chore and an intrusion, approach it as a privilege and an opportunity to engage in an activity that allows you to express yourself creatively.

Instead of thinking of retirement as the absence of work, think if it as the ability to engage in activities that are fulfilling to you. Don't buy into the belief system that says that you're a valid, worthwhile individual only if you work all the time. In fact, discard the labels of "work = bad" and "play = good," and fill your life instead with *activities* that have value for you, and that have no attached belief systems.

I'm putting in as many hours now as I did twenty years ago, working harder than my children would like me to, and in my mind I have been retired for a long, long time.

RETIREMENT

Retirement is when we do what we want to do.
Work is NOT important. It's just the place
where we spend most of our lives.

There are basically two types of activity:
WORK, and PLAY.

Tiger Woods and golf: Work? Or play?
Mark McGuire and baseball: Work? Or play?
Great artists and their art: Work? Or play?
Commercial fisherman and fishing:
Work? Or play?
Doctors and healing: Work? Or play?

When I use the word "play," it's serious.
Games are very, very serious.

There are more TV programs, books,
conversations, and talk shows about games
than about work.
If there were TV shows about work, nobody
would watch them!

GAMES ARE SERIOUS.
Do you know why we love games?
It's because of the rules.

When we play a game, we unconsciously adopt
the following objectives and rules:
1. Win!
2. Explore the possibilities.
3. Seek challenges.
4. Find out how good we can be.
5. Try out equipment, tactics, strategies.
6. We don't want the game to end, and when it
   does, we play again as soon as possible.
7. We never "fail" at a game -- we just win or
   lose. There's always another chance.

When we work the rules are different:
1. Get comfortable.
2. Make it predictable.
3. Settle for average.
4. Don't fail.
5. Be reasonable.

Perhaps there should be no "work" versus
"play." Instead, only "activities," to which we
apply 2 different sets of rules.
The rules we apply to an activity determine
how well we engage and how much we enjoy it.
Intuitively successful people use only 1 set of
rules in everything they do: GAME rules. They
want to WIN... at being a parent, at the office,
in relationships, etc.

The next time you're in a fast food restaurant, I want you to study the expressions on the faces, and the body language, of the people working behind the counter. I think you'll see the same things I do, and it tells you this about those people:
In most cases they're not happy.
They're making minimum wage.
They feel pressured.
They rarely smile.

Keep looking, and in all likelihood you'll see one person who doesn't fit the mold. He or she is smiling, energetic, productive, and adding joy to the job—and to the lives of coworkers and customers.

What's wrong with this person? Doesn't he or she understand that this is a low paying, demanding, dead end job?

Quite the contrary.

That particular young person has a VISION of owning this franchise, and perhaps others like it. He or she wants to be the best french-frier, the best customer server, the best assistant manager, and the best manager that franchise has ever had. Technical proficiency is in his or her sights.

That young person intuitively understands that if he or she is really good at what he or she does, the money to buy the franchises will show up. While the rest of the staff is only "putting in time" for their inadequate paychecks, this one is on the way to becoming wealthy. This person is playing the game called WIN.

> It's not the time you put in that counts; it's what you put into the time.

What is truly sad is that all the employees are there for the same number of hours. It's not the time you put in that counts; it's what you put into the time.

In our society, most people "work" 40+/- hours per week—while they're unconscious, unhappy, and feeling stressed out.

You may be thinking, "Yeah, but this guy doesn't understand my [situation, boss, company]. No matter what I do, I'll never get [promoted, enough money, recognition, etc.]."

{ belief systems and options

{ possibility

Great! You'll just be the best at what you do. The world is looking for people who are the best at what they do. Your current employer isn't the only one in the world!

"It's not enough to reach for the brass ring. You must also enjoy the merry-go-round."

Julie Andrews

Chapter 6
Are You Playing Small?

In Chapter 3, we learned to discard the belief system that told us to start at the bottom, struggle and toil, and work our way up — an approach that never defines your vision; therefore it gives you no means of determining whether you're on course.

We learned, instead, to start at the top — start with a vision, let the plan materialize, and make adjustments along the way to ensure that you're aligned.

Because many people never identify their vision in life, they become trapped in the gerbil wheel that our belief systems have built for us. They believe that they are their jobs and their stuff. They work to make money, to become comfortable. They go unconscious. Bad things happen, knocking them back to survival mode, and they do the hard stuff all over again, around and around and around.

> Once you have a vision, a plan appears.
>
> Once you're conscious of a plan, an appropriate strategy become obvious.
>
> Once you've decided on your strategy, the daily tactics become apparent to you.

They *think small,* and as a result they live small.

It's not that they are "less" somehow than successful people — their intelligence and their creative potential may be every bit as great. But because they think small, the box they live in is tight and restrictive. They spend their lives exhausting themselves, getting nowhere.

On the next page, I've inserted a quotation by the Reverend Marianne Williamson, sent to me by a friend. I carry it with me and re-read it often, even though quite frankly it irritates me.

See if you can guess why.

"Our deepest fear is not that we are inadequate.
Our deepest fear is that we are powerful beyond measure.
It is our light, not our darkness, that frightens us.
We ask ourselves, "Who am I to be brilliant, gorgeous, talented, fabulous?"
Actually, who are you not to be?
You are a child of God.
Your playing small doesn't serve the world. There's nothing enlightened about shrinking so that other people won't feel insecure around you. We are all meant to shine as children do.
We were born to make manifest the glory of God that is within us.
It's not just in some of us, it's in everyone. And as we let our own light shine, we unconsciously give other people permission to do the same.
As we're liberated from our own fear, our presence automatically liberates others."

From A Return To Love:
Reflections On The Principles Of A Course In Miracles
by Marianne Williamson.
Harper Collins 1992. Chapter 7, Section 3: Page 190.

Did the same line bother you, too?

Your playing small doesn't serve the world.

It annoys me because it disturbs my comfortableness. It prods me. Because I am not an intuitively successful person, because I work at being successful, it is natural for me to want to stay where I am in life, where it's familiar and comfortable.

> "Your playing small doesn't serve the world."
>
> Marianne Williamson

But comfort is not why I am here, on this planet. I know this, even though it's safer, and more comfortable, to ignore it. That line, *Your playing small doesn't serve the world*, reminds me of this. Rev. Williamson is reminding me why I get out of bed every morning. She is telling me I cannot let "comfort" be my primary motivator if I am to achieve my *purpose*.

Do you know what your purpose is? Do you know why you get out of bed in the morning?

Let's go back to those tough questions you asked yourself at the beginning of Chapter 1.

1. Who am I?
2. Why do I get up every morning?
3. What am I trying to accomplish?

You should be better able to answer them now.

Who are you?
You are your vision.
You are your commitments.
You are the value of your word.

Why do you get up every morning?
You get up every morning to engage in activities that are consistent with your visions.

What are you intending to accomplish?
You are trying to make a difference in the world.

To make a difference in the world! That's a pretty big box in which to live.

Making a difference in the world is one of the most selfish things you can do. It will bring you:

√ Joy
√ Power
√ A sense of being ALIVE
         and, most likely,
√ Money.

Don't believe what you just read. Try it, and see what happens in your life.

Meanwhile, did you notice how it made you feel to consider that you might be capable of making a significant difference in the world?

If you're like most people, you're saying, "Who, me? I'm too young! (or too old, or I'm the wrong sex, or I went to the wrong school, or I was born on the wrong side of the tracks, or I'm not clever enough....)."

I'll bet you're having one of two reactions to this notion. You're either thinking, "Oh, what a wonderful, generous, and kind philosophy," or you're thinking, "What a load of spiritual junk!" The truth is, making a difference is neither lofty nor burdensome. It's purely practical, and the payback is huge.

> Do not believe me. Do it yourself. Prove me wrong. Decide for yourself whether it works.

Make A Difference In The World

Almost sounds arrogant, doesn't it?
Here are some examples of how to do it.

Read a book to a child. Recognize someone who helps you. Put a dollar in a charity collection box. Be supportive of one person each day. Do something nice, just for the sake of surprising someone else. Let that driver who's trying to switch lanes get in front of you. Create a support group for parents of disturbed children. Organize a fund raiser for your house of worship. Volunteer to create a food collection program for needy people. Run for public office. Start your own business. Create a new political party that represents your principles. Pull together a group to build a new hospital.

The key is to start. Start where you are today. I'll tell you a secret: making a difference is addictive. Once you get hooked, you'll keep expanding, getting more excited about seeing more possibilities.

Who am I?

I'm a person who makes a difference.

Here's the problem.

Playing small is comfortable. And unless you're intuitively successful, playing small is a habit that requires constant diligence to overcome. My irritation at being reminded of it is akin to the irritation you might feel if someone repeatedly nudged you when you started dozing off.

But ultimately I am grateful for the nudge. I don't want to sleep through life. My playing small doesn't serve the world. Nor does yours.

Intuitively successful people play big. They are motivated by vision. They are clear about their commitments. And they do not allow themselves to become immobilized by the idea of moving out of their comfort zone.

Success is well within reach for the rest of us, as long as we have the insight, the awareness, and the strength of character to not allow someone else's belief systems to dominate our lives, and as long as we are willing to wake up, step out of our comfort zone, and keep moving upward.

Chapter 7
You Do Not Need To Get Fixed.

How do you think about yourself? Unconsciously, you have chosen to be in one of two spaces in life, and which space you're in will have a profound effect on how far you go, how much you struggle, and how successful you are.

Space Of Being is a psychologist's term. It applies easily to each of us, whether we have to work consciously at success, or are intuitively successful. Your Space Of Being signifies your fundamental point of view, the position from which you view the world. You are either *At Cause*, or *At Effect*. A "do-er" or a "let-er". Pro-active or Re-active. The label isn't important. It just describes the position.

I believe 97% of the people we associate with each day are At Effect. Only 3% are At Cause. All the successful people I've met, worked with, or read about, have been At Cause. The terms may be somewhat alien, but the concept is quite simple.

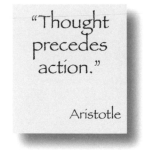

"Thought precedes action."

Aristotle

> "It is not the strongest of the species that survive, nor the most intelligent, but the one most responsive to change."
>
> Charles Darwin

Most people are unconscious most of the time. This is not to say they are dullards, or uneducated—they may be quite intelligent and learned, they may have done very well in school. They may have college degrees, and well developed vocabularies.

We are surrounded, every day, by bright people, who nevertheless live most days in an unconscious state. And, without realizing it, they announce to the world that they are At Effect, by some simple words they select from those big vocabularies, to use in their everyday language. Those words, which I'll describe in a moment, also tell you exactly what these people are planning to do, in all honesty, even if they themselves are not aware of their plans. And ironically, the only people who are listening to this potentially valuable information are the 3% who are At Cause. They're the people who play the game of Ask-And-Listen. They're the intuitively successful, along with those rare individuals who are consciously successful.

People who are At Effect use the word "hope".

"I hope I get more money."
"I hope my relationship with
my spouse improves."
"I hope the family starts getting
along better."
"I hope I'm able to lose 15
pounds."
"I hope I'll be successful."

What's wrong with *hope*?

Nothing, if you don't expect results.
You can sit down and *hope really hard*,
and nothing will change. To *hope* that
something will change is to relinquish
all your power, to put all your *hopes*
into the hands of some external force.
When you say you *hope* something
will happen, you are announcing to
the world that you intend to take no
action yourself. Your intention is to
be passive, immobile.

Another word At-Effect people use is
"try".
"I'll try to make it to your
dinner party."
"I'll try to get the work done."
"I'll try to pick you up on
time."

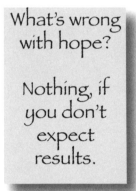

What's wrong
with hope?

Nothing, if
you don't
expect
results.

People try very hard, they really do. There is only one problem with trying hard: Nobody is interested in how hard you try; the results are all that matter. But, we operate on a belief system that says that trying, in and of itself, is a valiant, noble thing. Even if you accomplish nothing. We have become addicted to trying hard, running faster on the gerbil wheel. Even if we get nowhere, we can be proud of the fact that we tried hard. The trying, the exertion, becomes its own reward, and we can fall into bed at night feeling validated.

Well, guess what? No one cares how hard you try.

Results are what counts.

Hope is helpless.

Do not try. Either do, or do not.

This was a very difficult concept for me to accept. It felt cruel, and lonely, and heartless. There are a lot of people in our society who try very hard, and never get anywhere. Their suffering is painful to see. It isn't fair.

It is empowering, though, to realize that this is, simply, the way it is. You

"Do or do not, Luke. Do not try."

Yoda

can't change it — the world would go broke if it rewarded everybody who tried hard, regardless of their productivity. You either produce results, or you don't. What is, is. Now: What are you going to do about it?

One phrase At Effect people use constantly is "have to". The "have-to's" in their lives are the reasons, they say, that they can't have the life they want. I would disagree. There is very little, if anything, in your life, that you have to do.

"I have to commute to and from work, 3 hours a day."

No, you don't! You make that commute because you are committed to a certain quality of life for your family. Every day, when you make that commute, you are making a great gift to them.

"I have to work 60 hours a week."

No, you don't! You are working to provide the people you love with a standard of living that they otherwise would not enjoy. You're giving them a gift every day.

> It is empowering to realize that this is, simply, the way it is.
>
> What is, is.

"I have to devote 16 hours a day to taking care of my family."

No, you don't! You are giving your family a gift of a loving, caring parent every day.

These activities most likely will not change. What you CAN change is your perception of the activities.

A "have to" is a burden that will grind you down. There is no freedom, joy, love, or satisfaction in a "have to".

A "choice" is a very different thing. It gives you power, energy, and joy. It's not really what you do that determines your happiness.

It's your attitude and your perception about what you do.

Let's compare 2 hard-working people. They're at the same job, working the same hours.

Ned wakes up and says, "Another crummy day at the same rotten office."

Sandy wakes up and says, "I wish I didn't have to go to work today. However, I can see the results of my

"It's never too late to be who you might have been."

George Eliot

90

efforts in the life I've provided for my family. Therefore, I <u>choose</u> to go to the office.

Choices give you power. You can stay in bed! If you stay in bed every day, you'll probably lose your job, and you won't "have to" go there any more. Problem solved, right?

Or, you can go to work and congratulate yourself for honoring your commitment to providing for your family. You can feel good about yourself. The truth is, we don't give ourselves enough credit for acting with integrity in our daily lives.

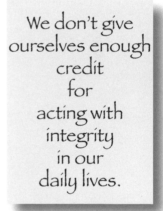

We don't give ourselves enough credit for acting with integrity in our daily lives.

Three bricklayers were working side-by-side. A man asked the first bricklayer what he was doing. He replied, "I'm laying bricks. It's a tough job."

The man asked the second bricklayer the same question. He replied, "I'm building a brick wall."

The third bricklayer, when asked the same question, said, "I'm building a cathedral."

From a distance you'd say the three men were doing the same job. But were they?

Which do you think enjoys his work the most?
Which do you think is the better bricklayer?
Which of them is pursuing a vision?

As we go through life, we are all required to do some things we might prefer not to do.

If your choice is to engage in an activity because you "choose to" as part of the process which will enable your visions to come true, your attitude and your performance will be totally different than if you engage in the activity as a burden which you "have to!"

You are free to choose:
> Your attitude
> What you do
> Whether you do it
> How you do it

That sounds to me like a lot of choices. Give yourself the credit you deserve. You are important, the activities you have chosen do impact the people around you. You make a difference because of your choices.

Another word At-Effect people use is "someday". And these words: "could... should... might....maybe."

"I'll deal with that problem *someday*... I *might* be able to get it done.... *Maybe* I'll do it tomorrow. "

Can you hear the lack of commitment in these words? The lack of movement? What do you think are the odds the problem will be resolved?

When is a good time to resolve problems? Problems crop up all the time, every day.

At-Cause people deal with whatever shows up, when it shows up. At-Effect people let things stack up, and before long there's too much to do, and not enough time to get it all done. Who created that stack? They did. It weighs them down, knocks them off course. They are busy talking themselves out of corners, giving excuses for falling short. Their gerbil wheel spins and squeaks, and they never move from the place where they started. It's a noisy, cluttered, frustrating world.

"Hey Yogi,
do you
know what
time it is?

"You mean,
now?"

At-Cause people live in the world of *now*, not *someday*. They travel light. *Yes* and *no*, not *maybe*. *Count on me. I'll be there.* You either *do*, or *do not*. It's a quieter world, a world of integrity, where fewer words are spoken and each one has value.

The At-Effect world is an emotional world. At-Effect people are always upset, because somebody or something is always to blame for their plight. "You wouldn't *believe* what happened to me!" (But they tell you anyway.) They choose to emote — to kick and scream, to cry, to rant, to complain. They tell you all the details, all the excuses for their failure to measure up, all the nitty gritty little problems that stopped them in their tracks. They do this because they operate on the mistaken premise that they are the only people on earth who meet with frustrations and distractions, and you are interested in hearing all about it, rather than in seeing real results. So vast is their arrogance, in fact, that they believe *everybody* cares about them.

They live in *A world full of sound and fury... signifying nothing.* (Shakespeare)

I have learned an enormous truth about this emotional mindset that has set me free. It is one of the most exciting, liberating, positive things anyone will ever tell you. And, if you're like me, for a few days it'll leave you feeling a little lonesome:

NOBODY CARES.

It seems like a terrible, pessimistic viewpoint, and when I realized how true it is, I was filled with resentment.

Then, the more I played with it, the more it empowered me. It is not a paranoid point of view, it is a position of freedom. In fact, it sets your life up in such a way that you can be met with almost continuous joy and happiness. Here's one reason why.

When you believe everybody cares, you believe you can count on everybody to listen to you, take an interest in your problems, and help you.

You have, in other words, expectations. Strings attached. But think back to all the disappointments,

> ## "NOBODY CARES"
>
> It's not a negative concept. I'm not saying, "Expect the worst." I'm saying, "Expect what shows up."

frustrations, anger, and resentments you carry around with you. Trace them back to the source. Most result from a thwarted expectation. You thought someone was going to do something, but they let you down. You thought it would be done in a certain way, but it wasn't. You thought it would be done on time, but it was late.

When you let go of all your expectations, you will *never* be disappointed. In fact, there are many people who really *do* care about you and me. There even are perfect strangers who will go out of their way to do marvelous things for you.

And, because you no longer *expect* this, because you no longer rely on others for your needs, your days will be filled with pleasant surprises. There is no chance for disappointment: only joy, warmth, and happiness. Your response is to say, "Thank you! That was wonderful! I didn't expect that! I appreciate it!" You give away *recognition*, and everybody gets to be happy.

Believing that Nobody Cares is how a person learns to Take Responsibility. In our society, the word *responsibility* is as off-putting as the word *commitment.* Our belief system tells us that responsibility is a burden. We're saddled with it. We're roped into it. It's a cage, a prison, a ball and chain. It's a liability, so most people go out of their way to avoid it. They understand that they can't say "It's not my fault" if they're responsible!

But here's the catch: Being responsible is the only way you can be At Cause.

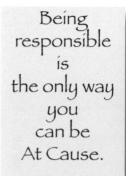

The successful 3% At-Cause crowd cheerfully take responsibility for everything in their lives. This not only empowers them and sets them up for pleasant surprises, it also keeps them out of that no-win situation called the Blame Game. *Responsibility is freedom and power.*

One of the great belief systems we were raised with is so pervasive and so alluring that it does untold damage in our lives. It is
the myth of 50-50.
Although it's an improvement over the philosophy that we should take responsibility for nothing, it's still off the mark.

The myth of 50-50 tells us that we should take 50% of the responsibility for getting whatever we want in life. The assumption is that something or somebody will show up and provide the other 50%.

Sounds fair, right? Perhaps. But this approach has killed many marriages, business partnerships, employee reviews, and friendships. Here's why.

When you enter into any relationship while carrying the myth of 50-50, you are not committed to that relationship. Rather, you're committed to keeping score.

> When you enter any relationship with the myth of 50-50, you are not committed to that relationship. You are committed to keeping score.

You notice when your significant other is contributing "only 45%" — and what's the knee-jerk response to such a revelation? (WHO DOES SHE [or he] THINK SHE [or he] IS?) You pull back, start giving only 40%. Your partner notices you're doing less, and s/he does what? FEELS RESENTFUL. Pulls back to 35%, and feels quite justified in doing so!

I'm sure you can see that this is not an approach that fosters healthy relationships; this is an approach that keeps divorce lawyers in Armani suits.

Instead, just as you commit to taking full responsibility for your life, *commit to 100% in all your relationships*, whether you're dealing with a business relationship, a tennis partner, or a spouse. Approach the relationship as though you were willing to live with 100-0, rather than 50-50.

Expect nothing, in other words.

Is it fair? Of course not. And if the relationship turned out to be 100-0, you eventually would want to re-evaluate its value. But by approaching it 100-0, you are obeying the third of those three immutable laws of success we talked about in Chapter 2:

Add Value.

If the relationship is important to you, this approach works every time. You see, one thing age and experience have taught me is that what's *fair* is vastly less relevant than what *works*. I am interested in what produces the results, what keeps me on the path to my vision, to which I am committed.

Put another way, let's say you have an intimate relationship with a significant

> What's fair is vastly less relevant than what works.

> "It is a wretched taste to be gratified with mediocrity, when the excellent lies before us."
>
> Isaac D'Israeli

other, and you both agree to the 50-50 rule. If you both are diligent about putting in your 50%, what is the most the relationship will ever give you? Well, 50 + 50 is 100%.

That may sound attractive, but 100% is what you could achieve by yourself, without a significant other. What good is that?

If, instead, you both agree to add value, to the tune of 100-100, and are both diligent about giving your all, what is the most the relationship will yield? 100 + 100 = 200%. That's the kind of relationship that gives fabulous returns. You'd have to agree, you're much better off in a relationship that doubles your investment, than in a relationship that gives you no more than you could get all alone.

Even if your partner puts in only 35% while you put in 100%, you're still in a relationship that's made your life better than it would have been if you were alone. And, because your objective is to *Add Value*, to live by the rule of 100-0, to take what you want and give it away, you are 100% aligned with your vision in doing so.

100

If you were to sort through all the characteristics of the At-Effect crowd and pick the one that sums up their philosophy of life, what would it be? Here's my vote:

"I wish things were different."

If you were to sort through all the characteristics of the At-Cause crowd and pick the one that sums up their philosophy of life, it would be this:

"What is, is. What is not, is not."

At-Effect people believe that most of what happens in life, and most of what they do, are dictated. They *have* to endure these occurrences, these hardships, this job.

At-Cause people believe we are free to make choices every minute of every day. The only things you absolutely *must* do in life are maintain 98.6° F body temperature, consume about 2000 calories of nourishment and about 8 ounces of water per day, and sleep.

Everything else is a choice.

"You cannot always control what goes on outside.
But you can always control what goes on inside."

Wayne Dyer

Being Right

Because successful people take full responsibility, they accept the consequences for every decision they make. There always are consequences.

By accepting full responsibility, you let go of your attachment to being *right*.

The need to be right is another one of our culture's belief systems — we're discouraged from ever owning up to our mistakes, for fear we'll be punished, sued, thought less of, laughed at, or knocked down a notch.

All these consequences are possible, but the worse choice would be to conceal our mistakes and disavow the consequences for the decisions we've made. Instead of unburdening ourselves of the baggage for each of those "secrets," we plunk each rock, one after another, into our backpacks and carry the burden around.

Thus laden, we guarantee we'll never get as far in life as our potential would have made possible.

Think about the last heated argument you had. Who won?

> "Our self image and our habits tend to go together. Change one and you will automatically change the other."
>
> Maxwell Maltz

Are you <u>sure?</u>

If you think the other person won, think again. Even if he or she was 100% right, how do you feel about him or her since that argument? A little bit resentful? It's human nature. The truth is, the next time you have an opportunity to interact with that person, there's a strong chance you'll give a little less, make a somewhat less attractive offer, be less generous. So, who won? Nobody did.

Go back to that argument again for a moment. Let's say you're sure you're right, and you could easily win. Knowing what you do about how "losing" makes you feel, why not concede the argument? Most "right versus wrong" arguments are not about things that really make a difference. When faced with one of these confrontations, why not let the other person "win?" Use neutral phrases—"I understand your position....I see why you feel that way.... I understand how could arrive at that conclusion." Let go of your attachment to being right. There's no payoff for being "right". The payoff comes from producing results.

> "It often times serves us well to allow other people to be right. Sometimes it's all they have in life."
>
> Dostoyesfsky

People who live At Effect live in a world of scarcity, where there isn't enough love, time, or money. People who live At Cause live in a world of abundance, where there is more than enough of everything to go around.

People who live At Effect live in a world of scarcity. They feel, in essence, that there isn't enough. Not enough love, not enough time, not enough money. So, whenever anything shows up, they grasp it, hold it close, and hoard it. They're afraid that if they let it go, they'll never get it back. The belief system tells them, "Easy Come Easy Go." No one can convince them otherwise.

People who live At Cause live in a world of abundance. They feel there is more than enough of everything, and they are generous with it all: their time, their love, their money, their creativity. They have observed, and know to be true, the Law Of Abundance introduced in Chapter 4:

If You Think About What You Need Most In Life, And Give It Away, It Will Come Back To You Manyfold.

They know, through experience, that what they give away is returned to them in multiples.

Help

People who live At Effect ask for help often. They believe they need it. They believe they deserve it. They believe they are entitled to it.

People who live At Cause never ask for help, and never give it. This may sound harsh and self centered, but the opposite is true.

"Help" conveys motionlessness. When a person asks for help, he is at a dead stop. He wants to be picked up, dusted off, and given what he needs. Think of him as seated in a chair, and if you give him a little shove, he moves very little — he may lean a little, but he's still seated, and as soon as you let up, he goes back to his original position. What he thinks he wants is for you to expend considerable energy in order to get him up, get him started, guarantee results. Odds are, even if you do all of this, he will be dissatisfied. At the very least, he will need help again, very soon. Being the "helper" is a powerful position, and whatever power the "helpee" might have had before you stepped in is extinguished when you become involved.

> When people ask for help, they are at a dead stop. When they ask for support, they are already in motion.

TWO DIFFERENT WORLDS
The language and belief systems in the worlds of *at cause* and *at effect*

At Effect
Hopes, wishes, dreams
I will try
Someday
Maybe
I might, I could, I should
"Everybody cares"
Emotional, always upset
Expectations and disappointments
Help me
Avoid responsibility
Burdened
Trapped
Noisy, cluttered, argumentative
Fault, right vs. wrong, victim, blame
50-50
What should be, what shouldn't be
Scarcity
There is never enough, hoarding
"If only" — deny reality
Reasonable
Have to
Focus on efforting
A circular domain
"but" (denies what preceded it in a
sentence)
Nothing ever changes

LISTEN to yourself.
NOTICE the words you use.
BE open to the possibility that when you change your
words, your behavior will change.

At Cause

No hope, only results and commitment
Do, or do not
Now
Yes or No
Count on me, integrity, my word
"Nobody cares"
Calm
Pleasant surprises
Ask for, and give, support
Take full responsibility
Travel light
Free
Quiet, uncluttered
No victim, no blame
100-0
What is, is
Abundance
There is plenty, generous
Deal with reality as it exists
Visions
Choice
Focus on results
A linear domain
"and" (includes what preceded it in a sentence)
Heading towards a destination

NO VICTIMS HERE

On my way home from giving a presentation, I discovered in the airport lot that my car had a flat tire.

"All right, BD," I said to myself. "Are you going to lose it? Or practice what you preach?"

I spent a few seconds in the At Effect world, feeling sorry for myself. Then I chuckled, tossed my stuff into the back seat, and changed the tire.

When I finally got home, I hit the remote button and waited for the garage door to lift… and there was my wife's car, smack in the middle of the garage.

I laughed.

I love my wife.

She didn't do that to annoy me. She's not thoughtless. She probably had the grandkids in the car and had her hands full, and just left the car where it stopped.

It wasn't personal.

I am not a victim.

Support

People who live At Cause never ask for help, because they are rarely, if ever, at a dead stop. They may, however, ask for support from time to time. That's because they're already in motion, maintaining a momentum, and need only a little boost in order to pick up speed.

They also are very supportive of others who are At Cause, and they know enough about the exchange of power to know that giving *help* to someone who is immobile is not doing anybody any favors. Giving *support* to someone who is immobile is not likely to produce significant results. Compared to the person who is seated, at a dead stop, the amount of energy it takes to give a boost to someone who already is in motion is miniscule. And, by providing this support, you are not extinguishing their power. I guarantee that any energy you contribute to being supportive of a person who is At Cause will be repaid, with generous interest.

> "There are people who believe it can be done and there are people who believe it cannot be done. They are both correct."
>
> Henry Ford

Why would anyone choose to be At Effect?

The truth is, we all were born to live At Cause, in the linear world. We were born perfect. No one ever consciously does anything that is not in their own best interest.

We were *learned* belief systems that veered us off course. This was not necessarily a purposeful, vindictive process — many belief systems take root quite by accident. When a person enters the world of being At Effect, in most cases he or she is unaware that this has happened.

And, there are some insidious and addictive benefits to being there, making it increasingly difficult to lever oneself out:

1. There's a lot of company in that world. It's filled with people who reinforce that you're "right".
2. You can be emotional there — it is the norm.
3. You can avoid responsibility, and you're constantly reminded that this is the smart way to be.
4. You can avoid the "trap" of commitment.

Many belief systems take root quite by accident.

Belief Systems and
The Accidental Ham

Whenever a festive ham dinner was served in the Smith household, the butt of the ham was cut off before baking. Generation after generation, it was done this way until one of the great-grandsons got married, and his young wife asked the family matriarch about it. "Oh, I suppose I started it," she said. "My oven was too small to hold a whole ham, so I cut the butt off to fit it in." A practical solution to fit a specific situation had become a belief system about how to bake a ham.

> Everybody,
> even
> fabulously
> successful
> people,
> lives in both
> domains.
> The
> difference is,
> successful
> people
> minimize the
> time they
> spend in the
> At Effect
> world. You
> can, too.

5. You can never fail in the At Effect world, because you are a victim. Nothing is ever your fault.
6. You are encouraged to have great expectations of others, but place no expectations upon yourself — you can forget about contributing value and concentrate instead on extracting the most from the "system".
7. Victims dominate the world, so if misery loves company, you will be very well accompanied.

Take a look at the chart of language and beliefs on pages 106 and 107. If you can identify yourself in both domains — being At Effect with 97% of the population sometimes, and being At Cause with 3% of the population at other times— take heart: this is the way it is for all of us. We all live in both domains, even fabulously successful people. You may be cruising along in the linear world, At Cause with the 3%, when something happens and you suffer a setback. You slide into the world of living At Effect, crowded among the 97% on the gerbil wheel. I've spent a lot of time there in my life, enough to know my way around fairly well. Even now I am not consistently able to keep myself from making that slide when something happens in life to shove me off course.

The difference, over years of studying this material, is instead of spending two years At Effect, I now may limit it to only 20 minutes. Some people are there for only a moment or two. For the finest success in every aspect of life, learn to minimize the length of time you spend in the world of being At Effect. If you need a number, strive for spending less than 10% of your life there, in the circular domain.

To accomplish this, do you need to get your brain rewired? No. Do you need to go to lots of seminars? I don't think so — none of this is complicated enough to require intellectual support. Do you need to read a lot of books? Not unless you want to.
You see, you don't need to be "fixed". The truth is, you were born fixed.

How did I arrive at the conclusion that we were born fixed? What proof can I offer?

I offer you the greatest "learners" in the world: everybody in the world

For the finest success in every aspect of life, learn to minimize the length of time you spend in the world of being At Effect. Strive to spend less than 10% of your life there.

Victims Rule!

- They're the people who keep you busy.
- They're the people who cut you off on the highways.
- They're the people who are never prepared to pay the bill when you're waiting in line.
- They're the people who make you angry.
- They're the people who create consternation, anger, and confusion in your family.

Victims dominate this world.
And they're not going to change.

Do you know why they were placed on the planet?

To amuse us.

We have a choice. We can choose to be angry and frustrated by them, or we can merely notice their antics.

You don't have to go to the movies, read books, watch TV, or go to the theater any more. We are surrounded by all the drama and emotions anyone could want. The problem is, we insist that all their histrionics are "real life," rather than a show in which they're merely acting out a role they have chosen for themselves.

Victims spend their lives in one long, never-ending cocktail party. The problem is, we keep attending the party. Remember the last time you physically attended a real cocktail party?

I'll bet I can describe it:

- It was noisy.
- Everyone was expressing an opinion.
- There was a lot of energy floating around.
- People were arguing about their positions.

What is the end product of cocktail parties?

HEADACHES.

The cocktail party was never designed to be a forum in which to move anything forward. It is an occasion, to get into some conversations.

You keep attending VICTIMS' cocktail parties.
- They're exhausting.
- They're upsetting.
- They go nowhere.
- They take up a lot of your time and energy.

Here's how to avoid them, or at least minimize the time you spend at them, and minimize their effect on you.

- Don't treat them as "real." It's just a cocktail party. Don't get sucked in emotionally.
- Respond like this: "I understand your problem. What are you going to do about it?" [This will terminate the conversation!]
- Tell him or her that he or she is "right."

You see, victims don't want their problems solved. They want to talk about their problems. If you solve their problems, they'll come up with more of them to talk about.

under the age of 4 years. Go rent yourself a couple 4-year-olds. Let them LEARN you how to behave. They all live At Cause. They expect doing, not trying. They do not accept "try" as an answer. They live NOW. Tell a child that "someday" you'll take him to the circus, and notice his response.

Children are motivated by VISIONS. No child ever said he wants to grow up to be a clerk in a large corporation. Children all want to be astronauts, ballplayers, firemen, doctors.

Children are the ultimate pragmatic realists. They deal with what is.

They don't complain about the heat; they want to go swimming.

They don't complain about the snow; they want to go sledding.

They know all about what is, is.
You used to be a 4-year-old.
You know how to live At Cause.
You've lived there before, before it was learned and taught out of you.
We were born to live At Cause.

If you let go of the belief systems you were learned, what's left is CAUSE.

> No one needs to get "fixed". You were born "fixed".

> You know how to live At Cause. You've lived there before.

116

What holds us back from exploring possibilities?

• Fear of humiliation.
• Fear of failure.
• Fear that we're not good enough.
• Fear of embarrassment.

These are concepts a 4-year-old cannot grasp. These are concepts we were learned and taught. There isn't a 4-year-old on the planet who was born with them.

Failure is a concept children do not understand. If they did, you and I would still be crawling on hands and knees. Watch a child learn to walk. He'll fall a thousand times. I've never known a child to say, "I'm a failure at this walking thing," and quit. Each time they fall down, they get up.

Children are committed to everything they do.

> "Can we go to McDonald's?"
> "It's raining, dear."
> "I know. Can we go to
>   McDonald's?"
> "Dinner is in 1 hour."
> "I'll eat my dinner. Can we
>   go to McDonald's?"

"I have to clean the house."
"I'll help you! Can we go to
McDonald's?"

There isn't a 4-year-old on the planet
who thinks,
"I need a nose job."
"My ears are too big."
"I'm not smart enough."

You see, you were born fixed.
You used to live fixed.
You don't need to get fixed.

> The thing that drives you crazy about children is the very thing you need to get back.

The thing that drives you crazy about children is the very thing you need to get back. Children know what they don't know, and they're constantly asking questions and listening to the answers.

At birth, they're in survival mode. They can't even feed themselves. Four years later, they know colors, numbers, cars, airplanes, language, likes and dislikes, how to manipulate their parents.... How did they learn so much, so fast? By asking questions, being conscious, listening to answers, learning to do what works, and learning to stop doing what doesn't work.

Let's talk about this victim thing.

I realize my comments about "victims" will seem harsh to some readers. In our politically correct society it may jar their thinking and seem heartless.

There are individuals who truly need help. But let's look at the big picture. There are people who were born with severe "handicaps," and there are people who through no fault of their own are in dire emotional, psychological, or economic straits. They deserve support and, if needed, even help.

But this is not an escape hatch for anybody reading this book. Before any reader grasps at this description of handicap and uses it to excuse himself or herself from my critical comments about victims in this chapter, let me make a suggestion:

Go to a Special Olympics event. Watch so-called handicapped children compete. Notice their joy, their desire to win. Acknowledge the fact that they are out in the world, making things happen.

Come out to Winter Park, Colorado next winter and watch blind skiers schussing down the hill. Legless competitors in ski races. Skiers with one, or no, arms.

Read the bestselling books *Seabiscuit*, by Laura Hillenbrand, or *The Theory Of Everything*, by Stephen W. Hawking. These two authors are individuals who suffer from debilitating diseases.

And yet they are not debilitated.

One of the authors can move only one finger; he has no control over any other part of his body. The other has to spend weeks in bed after the slightest physical effort.

These people do not consider themselves to be victims.

Each is aware of the fact that the situation will never improve. Each has written a bestselling book. Each book is fabulous. And neither book makes mention of the author's handicaps anywhere in the text, acknowledgements, or dust cover.

That's because these people do not consider themselves to be victims. They are aware of the fact that they have more issues to deal with than you and I. They deserve all the support our society and we as individuals can bring to them.

Know, then, that when I speak or write about "victims" the way I have in this chapter, I am referring to people who choose to be victims.

You were born to live in the linear world. You were *learned* to live in the circular world. There is only one thing you need to do in order to maximize the time you spend in the quiet, serene, linear world, At Cause with the 3%:

LET GO.

Let go of your belief systems.
Let go of your attachment to being right.
Let go of excessive emotionality.
Let go of your fear of failure. Successful people fail all the time. The difference is, instead of saying, "I failed," they say, "It didn't work," and then they try *something different.*
Let go of the comfort of miserable company.
Let go of your need to dominate.
Stop thinking "I wish things were different," and start saying, "What is, is. Now what am I going to do about it?"

Successful people have established a vision. They are open to the possibilities that their vision will become reality — they don't tense up and try to "make it happen," they simply remain open to the possibilities. They are conscious. They notice when they veer off course, and they get themselves realigned. They do not assume that anybody will catch them veering; they take responsibility for monitoring their own progress.

Become conscious, stay that way, and let go of your belief systems, and you are back where you belong: In the linear world, At Cause.

With very few exceptions, success does not require extraordinary talent. All you need is to remember who you are:

You are your vision,

your commitments,

and your word.

Chapter 8
How To Get Less Busy And Have Everything You Want

We have been learned and taught that you can't be a success until after you get to the destination.

You can't be a success until <u>after</u> you have all the stuff – the money, the cars, the great relationships, the recognition, the houses, the clothes, etc.

You can't be a success until <u>after</u> you join the right groups, take the right trips, send your kids to the right schools, go to the right movies, eat at the right restaurants.

So, we use the following formula:

$$HAVE + DO = BE$$

But HAVE-DO-BE is an oxymoron. It cannot work. With this mindset, we picture ourselves as either wannabes or failures struggling to be successful.

Intuitively successful people use the same words for their formula, but in a different sequence:

They don't "end up" being anything — they <u>start out</u> being it.
They say, "I '<u>Be</u>' a success. Now, what are the appropriate things for me to <u>Do</u>?"

All athletes, intuitively successful people, and children, understand that BE + DO = HAVE is the way the world works. Olympic medalists don't become Olympic champions the moment they climb onto the platform and accept their medals. They became Olympic champions years before the competition took place, when they decided, "I '<u>Be</u>' an Olympic champion." Then, every day thereafter, they got out of bed and did what Olympic champions <u>Do.</u> They worked out, sought out competition, sought out the best coaches, and challenged themselves. That's how they ended up <u>have</u>-ing an Olympic medal.

> "Go confidently in the direction of your dreams. Live the life you have imagined."
>
> Henry David Thoreau

Michael Jordan did not become a superstar making tens of millions of dollars when he signed a multimillion dollar contract at age 21. He became a superstar when he was about 8 years old. He woke up and said, "I '<u>Be</u>' a superstar." For the next several years, he got up every day and did what superstars <u>Do</u> — he practiced his craft, got on teams, and at age 22 had superstardom.

Tiger Woods did not become, I believe, the greatest golfer in the history of the game when he won his first professional tournament. He became the greatest golfer in the world when he was 5 years old. You can see videotapes of the old Jack Paar show on television when he was interviewing little Elwood Woods. When Jack asked, "What are you going to <u>be</u> when you grow up?", little Elwood replied, "The greatest golfer in the world." What did he <u>Do</u>? He practiced his craft, took lessons, competed, won, lost, kept playing, and now <u>has</u> the reputation of being the greatest golfer in the world.

By the way, Tiger has no competition that I am aware of in pursuing his vision. Most professional golfers set their goals to be "in the top ten," or "winning a major," or "winning a lot of money." To my knowledge, Tiger is the only one committed to being the best in the history of the game. His vision is bigger than his present competition.

You can BE whatever you want to be, right now.

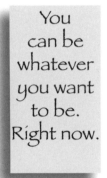

You can be whatever you want to be. Right now.

Shift from living your circumstances to living your visions. This takes only a nanosecond – that's 1/1000 of a second. The change takes place between your ears.

Take a look at your list of commitments. Here's an example, to make the point:

- To be a great dad.
- To never have to worry or even think about money.
- To make a difference in other people's lives.

What are *your* commitments?

Let's say one of them is to <u>Be</u> the best person in the world for someone to be in a relationship with.

Here's how to apply the formula.

1. Make a commitment to <u>be</u> exactly that.
2. Create three things that will reflect your commitments:
   a. Take that person out one night per week.
   b. Pleasantly surprise that person once a month.
   c. Listen to what he or she says.

Make a commitment to BE exactly what you want to be.

Will these three things make you the best person in the world to be in a relationship with?

NO.

What they will do, and this is no small thing, is start you down the path to HAVE-ing a great relationship.

That's all that's required:

START DOWN THE PATH.

> "When schemes are laid in advance, it is surprising how often the circumstances fit in with them."
>
> William Olsen

> "The longest journey starts with a single step."
>
> Confucious

Let's say one of your commitments is to be "the boss" at work. What are three things that will start you down that path?

1. Show up 5 minutes early every day.
2. Do just a little bit more than expected.
3. Be responsible — make your word good.

Will these things get you the boss's job? Probably not, but they will start you down the path.

Let's say you've committed to being financially independent. Start the process:

1. Pay $50 more per month on your credit card debt, and stop using credit to buy things you don't really want.
2. Learn about investing.
3. Go to night school one night a week to improve your skills.

Will these things make you financially independent? No, but they will start you down the path.

THE DOING-NESS MUST BE M-M-O.

Measurable

Monitorable

Observable.

Among other reasons for this, it will allow you to catch yourself doing the appropriate things, so you can reward yourself.

DO NOT TRY TO BE PERFECT. Perfection is what is keeping us from engaging in the process. The love of *perfection* leads to *procrastination*, which leads us to be *paralyzed.*

JUST START.

Start poorly.
Start badly.
Start being scared.
Start not being sure of the outcome.
Start being skeptical.

Just start.
Once you start, you are on the path. Amazing things will happen once you get on the path. Opportunities will appear, you will build momentum, it gets easier and

> Catch yourself doing the right things and reward yourself.

> "A life spent making mistakes is not only more honorable, but more useful than a life spent doing nothing."
>
> George Bernard Shaw

quicker. You will effortlessly start adding more and more DOingness.

First BE,

Then DO,

And you will

HAVE.

BE-DO-HAVE

"What a crazy idea…. Life can't work that way…. When is this guy going to get real?… He doesn't understand the pressure I'm under…. I'm too old…. It'll never work. Blah, blah, blah."

"Nothing happens in the universe unless something moves."
Albert Einstein

"What we think, or what we know, or what we believe, is, in the end, of little consequence. The only consequence is what we do."

John Ruskin

Do you see what's happening? Your belief systems have just jumped up to stop you.

Let's take a look at where this "crazy" BE-DO-HAVE idea came from.

The Christian Bible:
"As a man thinketh, so shall he be."

Eastern Philosophy:
The TAO (a concept over 2,000 years old): Be + Do = Have

Descartes: (agnostic French philosopher)
Cogito ergo sum. (I think, therefore I am.)

Gothae:
Before doing, one must be.

Plato:
To be is to do.

Socrates:
To do is to be.

These are just some of the examples of the fact that the great philosophers of all time, each in their own way, arrived at exactly the same conclusion.

How long is it going to take before you and I are open to the possibility that this is the way life works?

It's simple. It's not crazy. It's just different from the way we were programmed. And, that programming was installed after-market. We weren't born with it.

By the way, you cannot fail once you get on the path. The path is a process, not a destination. Therefore, there are only two possible outcomes:

"...do, be do be do...."

Frank Sinatra

1. You run out of time (die).
2. You achieve the objective.

What we have here, then, is a way of life, sponsored by the great minds of all time, which is failure-proof.

How good can it get?

BE + DO = HAVE is the path.

When is the right time to get on the path? Age 5.

Several years ago, a 30-year-old man told me how he got on the path when he was 5 years old. He was at home

132

with his mom when two naval officers appeared at the door. They were there to let the family know that his dad had been killed. He had been a naval pilot. He'd been shot down.

They were devastated. Friends appeared and for several hours the scene was emotional, sad, and heartbreaking.

Later that day, he noticed his mom sitting alone. He climbed on her lap and said, "It's okay, Mom, I'm going to take Dad's place and be a naval fighter pilot."

"Okay, Dad, I'm coming to say hello."

From that moment on, he knew exactly what to do.
Get good grades. Be an athlete. No drugs. No DUIs. Win an appointment to the Naval Academy.
The first time he strapped himself into the cockpit of an F-14 airplane he said aloud, "Okay, Dad, I'm coming to say 'hello.'"

On the path at age 5.

My dad got on the path at the age of 72.
He was a mounted policeman in New York City. A great rider, a guy who built boats in our backyard,

self reliant, quiet, strong, and very creative with his hands. I can't remember more than one occasion that he went more than 100 miles from New York City.

At age 72, he went to Garrison, Montana to visit my stepsister. He realized when he was there that he was meant to be a cowboy. It figures — look back at my description of him! So, at age 72, he moved from New York to Montana.

The happiest years of his life were from 72 to 94. He was a cowboy. He taught kids how to care for their animals, went to rodeos, learned to fish, got concerned about the price of cattle, went deer hunting. He was a cowboy.

On the path at age 72.

I'm not limiting you to the ages of 5 to 72 years. You can get on the path right now.

Seems like a good time to me.

We are all at some position on the PHASES OF BEING chart (see next page), moving in some direction in all aspects of our lives.

We can be heading for, or at, success in our personal lives, getting better at the games we play, or getting worse.

Everything is in motion all the time.

Intuitively successful people live from the phase of IMMINENT FAILURE and UP. This is important for you to bear in mind. Intuitively successful people are not always striving and achieving. This is particularly true after realizing a goal, vision, or success. They rest. They reward themselves and enjoy their success.

Invariably, however, ENTROPY starts to take its toll. Depending on how mired in inertia they've allowed themselves to become, they find themselves drifting down to the phase of IMMINENT FAILURE.

Nothing bad has happened. If you and I were observing them, we wouldn't notice any change. They're still happy, secure, and in good financial shape.

> "I feel sorry for the person who can't get genuinely excited about his work. Not only will he never be satisfied, but he will never achieve anything worthwhile."
>
> Walter Chrysler

PHASES OF BEING

(Creation of more success around you)
SUCCESS

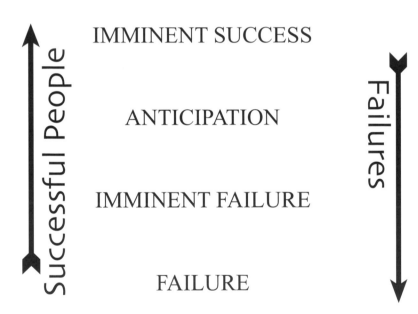

IMMINENT SUCCESS

Successful People

ANTICIPATION

Failures

IMMINENT FAILURE

FAILURE

(Creation of more failure around you)

Because they're conscious, though, they notice that they're comfortable. In fact, too comfortable. They're about to go unconscious. They're bored.

And so they change things, right then and there. They create new visions, challenge themselves, re-visit their commitments, and seek new ways to honor them. They move themselves into the phase of ANTICIPATION.

Which leads them back up to IMMINENT SUCCESS.

Imminent success is when you are engaged in activities that will lead to success, and the success hasn't shown up yet. When you're in IMMINENT SUCCESS, you will feel uncomfortable.

There are many advantages to being uncomfortable.
- You are conscious.
- You are alive.
- Your blood is pumping.
- You notice things.
- You are alert.

Not a bad way to go through life!

"Dispute the idea that you can achieve maximum human happiness by inertia and inaction or by passively and uncommitedly 'enjoying yourself.'"

Albert Ellis, Ph.D.

FAILURE: AN ANECDOTE

Several years ago, I walked past a basketball court and watched a 6- or 7-year-old boy attempting to hit the backboard on a basketball court with a regulation sized ball. He couldn't throw the ball high enough.
The ball would fall short, roll about 30 feet away, and he'd run and get it, race back in front of the hoop and throw it again. The ball would fall short, and he'd run and get it and throw it again.
One hour later, he was still at it.

The average adult would say the boy was failing.
I disagree.
He knew he was engaged in the

process of becoming a great
basketball player.

As adults, we "try" things. If we don't
get immediate results, we
conclude that we are "failures" and
give up. Children never give up until
they achieve the result or change their
commitments.

You and I were taught, and learned,
"DO NOT FAIL."

Left alone to pursue their dreams and
commitments, children never fail; they
just learn that it may take
longer and require more effort.
They know they are engaged in the
appropriate activities—they're on the
path.

They understand that as long as they
are on the path, there is no failure.
They're "in process".

Unsuccessful people live from the phase of IMMINENT SUCCESS and DOWN.

They are bright people. In most cases they know what to do to create success. They wake up one morning and say, "My life sucks. I'm going to change things," and they know exactly what to change.

> "Have no fear of failure. You'll never achieve it."
>
> Salvador Dali

They begin the process. They move into IMMINENT SUCCESS— anticipating all the good things that are going to happen.

They begin doing the right things, moving in the right direction, engaged in appropriate activities. Success is in their path.

However, they notice that they're uncomfortable. And, success hasn't shown up yet.

Because they're so attached to feeling comfortable, they stop engaging in the appropriate activities. They believe, "If this were the right thing to do, I'd feel comfortable."

And so, they go back to their old comfortable routines. They are now in the phase of IMMINENT

FAILURE. Unconscious, bored, and at the mercy of entropy. And, guess what: Something bad happens.

Life is no different for intuitively successful people than it is for the rest of us. The same bad and good things happen to everyone. Entropy applies universally. It does not discriminate.

The real issue is, when do you wake up, and are you committed to doing something about it?

Most people don't wake up until they're in FAILURE. Intuitively successful people see it coming and change something before they get to FAILURE.

The easiest, least stressful time to change is when things are good.

Counterintuitive, eh?

The fact is, you will change. Like it or not. The big question is, WHEN. After the "bad thing" has happened?

Or before?

The choice is yours.

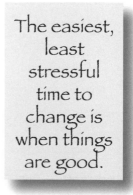

The easiest, least stressful time to change is when things are good.

HOW TO GET YOUR MIND TO SUPPORT YOU ON THE PATH

How many people does it take to hold a "cocktail party?"

One.

You and your little voice.

Have you noticed how much time you spend arguing with your little voice? Every time you begin exploring possibilities, it says,

- "Oh no you don't!"
- "You'll never do it."
- "We've tried this before and it's never worked."
- You'll embarrass yourself!
- Remember, your sister is the smart one.

And you start arguing.

Notice that your little voice rarely says,

"Go for it!"

Why is that?

142

Here's why.

Think of your mind as a computer. Computers are very fast and very dumb. Computers believe everything anybody puts into their databanks. Then, when we ask them questions, they give us answers based on what's been put in there.

So, if you program your computer to believe

$$2 + 2 = 6$$

then ask it to add 2 and 2, it'll tell you the answer is 6.

Your mind is the same way. It supplies answers based on the information put into it.

Computer experts have an expression for this: Garbage In, Garbage Out.

Most of us have minds (databases) filled with garbage, and we continue to shovel it in.

We hang out with Victims. Their information goes into the databank.

We listen to "garbage" music. The lyrics go into the databank.

We use Victim words ourselves:
Should have
Could have
If only
Try
Hope
...and the computer is so dumb, it puts our *own* "garbage" words back into the database!

We watch "garbage" entertainment. It all goes into the databank.

What do you think would happen if we consciously started putting "good stuff" into the databank? I'll tell you what: You'll start getting better information back out of the "computer".

How do we fill the databank with good stuff? There are three different techniques.

1. Cognitively
   a. Read "positive" books
   b. Watch "positive" movies
   c. Attend "positive" programs
   d. Where possible, avoid Victim "cocktail parties".

e. Stop using Victim words in your own speaking.

2. Reward, reward, reward yourself! Every time you catch yourself doing positive, reward yourself. The computer is so dumb, it notices you getting rewarded frequently and starts changing its opinion of you.

3. Model. Just "hang out" with people who have the skills, talents, and quality of life to which you aspire. Go looking for them. They're out there. The computer (mind) will absorb all their actions and words, and store that valuable information in the databank for you to draw upon. It is not necessary to "study" these people, or ask them a lot of questions, although you may choose to do so. I'm suggesting, however, that you merely be around them. The computer records everything 24/7 and believes it all. Have you noticed that losers hang out with losers, and winners hang out with winners? That's because winners

Just "hang out" with people who have the skills, talents, and quality of life to which you aspire. Go looking for them. They're out there.

know, intuitively, that by surrounding themselves with winners, somehow their own lives are happier and more productive.

"Birds of a feather flock together."

Grandma

That's all there is to it. If you overload your computer (mind) with good stuff, you'll discover that the garbage rule holds:

Good stuff in: Good stuff out. Garbage in: Garbage out.

You can't shut the little voice up.

You can, however, change what it says.

Chapter 9
Path Map

This chapter is a quick-reference map to help you stay on course. Use it when you need a reminder of your goals and purpose, when something happens to divert you, when you've slipped into the At Effect world, or when you feel you've become misaligned.

Step 1
Create Your Destinations

Give yourself the 10-Minute Gift.
Create 10 uninterrupted minutes, put aside your belief systems, and write down everything you want in life and out of life.

Circle the items that excite you, the ones that make you smile, the ones that bring you joy.

Good. Now you know where you are going.

DO NOT TRY TO FIGURE OUT HOW YOU ARE GOING TO GET THERE.

Step 2
Stay Conscious

Notice things. Notice when opportunities present themselves to you — opportunities that will take you down the path toward your destinations. Don't expect a new job offer, to win the lottery, or to suddenly re-invent your life. Merely be conscious of what appear to be "little things" that will make the journey possible.

If you want to be a better parent, for example, notice that your children look sad. Sit down, hug them, and let them know how you feel. Give them a chance to tell you how they feel, too.

The next time you're given an assignment at work, say, "Thanks!" (even though you might not feel thankful) and look for one good thing for you in that task. Reward yourself for your behavior. (See The Technology of Rewarding, page 160.)

If you want less stress and anger in your life, step back and look at the scene from an unemotional viewpoint. For example, say someone cuts in front of you in a line, or takes your parking place, or says something negative. Don't get angry. Why let them control your life? If you really want to get aligned, smile! Reward yourself for your behavior.

Watch yourself carefully. Reward yourself every time you notice that your behavior or reaction is consistent with your visions.

Step 3
Plant Seeds Of Behavior

Create 3 to 5 simple, relatively easy, observable, monitorable, measurable actions that are consistent with each of your visions.

Each time you notice yourself doing one of these things, reward yourself. (See The Technology of Rewarding, page 160.)

Tell at least one other person what your intentions are. It's really not important who you tell. What is important is that you hear yourself giving life to your intentions.

Don't attempt to be perfect.
Don't subject yourself to stress over this activity.
Don't beat yourself up. The world will provide all the punishment you need, and more.

Monitor yourself regularly. Each time you catch yourself off course — for example if your integrity is offline, or your actions are not aligned with your objectives — merely get back on course and "clean up" your transgression. Notice that when something like this happens, your belief systems attack you full-force. They'll say things such as,

> "I knew I couldn't do it!"

> "There I go, screwing up again!"

"None of this is really important…"

"I'm not good enough to do this."

You may not be able to stop these thoughts — the programming is too strong. Don't try to deny them or argue with them. Just let them be and GET BACK ON THE PATH. Let your behavior speak for you.

Over time, your intrusive, argumentative belief systems will appear less frequently and be less emotionally charged, but at first they're likely to be loud, hurtful, and frequent. Give them no power — intrinsically they have no power of their own, only that which you give them. If, at the start, you let them have zero impact on your behavior (even if they're persistent and disturbing), they'll lose some of the power you've given them in the past. Each time you accomplish this, they become less and less potent.

What a fantastic, joyous, freeing way to go through life!

Step 4
Remember:
NOBODY CARES

Expect NO SUPPORT on your journey.

Don't expect the best, or even the worst.

Expect NOTHING from other people.

The fact is, many people *will* support you on your
journey.
Stay conscious and notice the things other people do for
you.

BE SURE TO THANK THEM, AND MEAN IT.
When in doubt, overdo it!

Notice their reaction to your appreciation and
recognition.

Notice how YOU feel each time you acknowledge
someone else.

Step 5
Stay In The Present

Notice how much time you spend in the PAST or the FUTURE. That is all wasted time. Learn to ask yourself, "What am I doing right now?"

If what you're doing *isn't* moving you toward your visions,
STOP DOING IT!

If you're in a deep hole, stop digging!

If what you're doing *is* moving you toward your visions,
KEEP DOING IT! And, REWARD YOURSELF!
(See The Technology of Rewarding, page 160.)

Sounds easy, doesn't it.
It isn't easy, it's just SIMPLE.

If you stay with it, within 28 days or so, alignment will become your new habit.

Step 6
Deal With What Is

Let go of what "should" or "shouldn't" be.
Let go of how other people "should" behave.

What is, is.

What is not, is not.

Let go of "if onlys" and deal with what is.

Step 7
Explore Possibilities

Ask more questions and develop your listening skills. Be open to the possibility that there are possibilities. Notice things. Use the magic question:

"What would it take for me to _____

_____?

(fill in the blanks)

Notice the question: It doesn't say "What do I have to do... What would she/he/they have to do....?" The question is squarely in the realm of possibilities.

Notice that the first knee-jerk answer that will appear when you complete a "What would it take?" question will be "It can't be done." Just live with the question. Write it down. Look at it once in a while.

The answer will appear.

I don't know how this works. It just does. In most cases, the answer will amaze you. It will be an answer within your capabilities. It will present you with a walkable path.

Step 8
Slow Down

Focus on your visions and commitments.

Stop doing things that do not support these very important issues.

Be conscious of the amount of time, effort, and energy you invest in things that aren't important relative to your visions.
Protect your time. Use it exclusively to engage in activities that are consistent with your visions.

We live in a society that has learned us to be busy.
We're all running around with a beeper, two cell phones and a laptop. We're BUSYBEBACKS* — "I'm busy… I'll be back!"

Analyze if all this busy-ness is adding to productivity.

You'll be amazed at what you discover.

(*From *The Tao Of Pooh*, by Benjamin Hoff)

> "I hate to answer the telephone.
> Almost every time I do, there's
> someone on the other end."
>
> Fred Couples

Step 9
Be-Do-Have

Resolve to BE whatever you want to be, right now.

Look at your list of commitments and focus on each item, one at a time.

Commit yourself to BE whatever it is that each vision requires.

Support that commitment by making a list of 3 things you will do, for each item on your list, that will reflect and support that commitment.

Be conscious of the results.

Step 10
Stretch Yourself

One of the first things we want to do when we have a new car is find out how fast it will go. It's not that we intend to drive at this speed—we just want to know what the car's capabilities are.

It's nice to know how much power you have, even if you don't use it.

Set up a day to find out how much you can accomplish at work, during normal hours.
Think about the day.
Organize the day.
Refuse to be distracted.

Use this day to find out how good you really can BE.
Don't do it for the boss.
Don't do it to impress anyone.
Do it for yourself.

Set up a day to be the best person to be in a relationship with.
Don't tell the other person.
Think about the day.
Organize the day.
Execute the day.

Identify another vision, and do it all again.

Put the accelerator pedal to the floor (not on your car!) and see how powerful you really are.

You'll feel exactly the same sensation that you experience when you stand up and stretch, after being idle or cramped up.

You'll feel both exhilarated, and relaxed.

You will probably learn something about yourself. You'll gain an insight into your real capabilities and possibilities.

Step 11
Enjoy The Process

Most of life involves the process of getting somewhere. How long does it take to get a college degree? Thirty seconds. That's how long it took you to walk up the steps and receive your diploma.

But the process itself took four years.

Did you enjoy those four years?

How long will it take for you to achieve your visions? A week? Six months? Ten years? A lifetime? Does it really matter?

The key is to enjoy the process. The trip. The journey.

We've been taught as well as learned that you don't deserve a reward or recognition until you've completed the process.

I disagree.

Reward yourself for being in process.

Life is a game.
We all die at the end.
You will reach this finish line... everybody does.
Enjoy the process. Give meaning to each day.
Take care of yourself and the people you love.

Enjoy the journey.

The Technology of Rewarding

In this book I've repeatedly suggested that you reward yourself. In fact, I indicated that this cannot be overdone — there is no such thing as rewarding yourself too frequently. It's true.

What is a reward? I'll give you some examples.
Going for a nice walk.
Calling up a friend to say "hello".
Buying an ice cream cone.
Taking a long, hot shower or bath.
Spending five whole minutes looking at a flower.
Checking a book out of the library.
Renting that movie you've wanted to see.
Writing a note to your mom and dad.

I'm not talking about buying more stuff, particularly if that would mean going into debt or otherwise veering off course. Rather, make up a l-o-n-g list of "little" things that give you pleasure, and dip into that list often, to reward yourself for all the little vision-oriented victories you're going to make.

Reward yourself—no one else will!

If you would like more information about Bob
and his products, go to his website:

http://www.bobdunwoody.com

WHAT IS, IS.

NOBODY CARES.

BE + DO = HAVE

SOUNDS
CRAZY...

...MIGHT WORK!!!

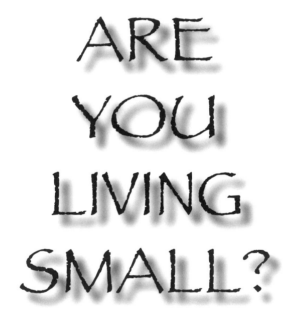

ARE
YOU
LIVING
SMALL?